RECYCLING CHRISTMAS CARDS

Eco Craft Projects and Ideas To Repurpose Holiday Cards

With 45 Special Blank Templates Included

ANNEKE LIPSANEN

PUBLISHERS NOTES

You may sell the genuine handmade crafts you make. The craft templates themselves may not be sold, distributed or used to create new books or digital or printable crafts. The book may not be sold, shared, or given away for free.

DISCLAIMER

No part of this publication may be reproduced, or transmitted in any form without prior written permission from Anneke Lipsanen.

The author, publisher, and distributor of this book assumes no responsibility for the use or misuse of this product, or for any injury, damage and/or financial loss sustained to persons or property as a result of using this book. The liability, negligence or otherwise, from any use, misuse or abuse of any instructions or ideas in the book is the sole responsibility of the reader/ crafter.

DEDICATION

This book is dedicated to frugal crafters, creative recyclers and everybody interested in the innovative repurposing of consumer goods.

I had so much fun making these projects and so will you! You will also find that you get new ideas as you go along. It is not just about recycling Christmas cards, but about recycling Christmas fun all year long! Get started now for the next Holiday season - for fun or profit.

If you enjoyed the book, please do leave a review, and blog and talk about it if you think other crafters will enjoy these Eco crafts and templates.

Recycle, Reuse, Reduce, Rethink, Remake, Repurpose!

WHAT THIS BOOK IS ABOUT

In this book you will find 50 fun craft projects to turn used Christmas and Holiday cards into charming new items. Make these projects for yourself, or to give away as unusual and thrifty gifts, packs, stocking stuffers and favors. You can also sell your crafted projects at craft markets, school or church fetes, fundraiser events for retirement centers, children's playschools and more. There are projects for packets, containers, table décor, walls and scrapbooking. The projects include 45 special templates that are sized and adapted for greeting cards. They are at the back of the book to trace off or photocopy, and for your convenience, are also provided as downloads. An extra printable set is entirely blank for even more paper crafts. They can be enlarged or reduced to fit different card sizes. There are bonus projects and printable papers too.

I wish you happy crafting.

Anni

TABLE OF CONTENTS

GETTING ORGANIZED

Get your equipment, cards and templates ready. The more organized you are, the more you can concentrate on the creative process.

The projects are rated as *Very Easy, Easy, Takes Time* and *Tricky*

WHAT YOU NEED

- A stash of used Christmas and Holiday cards
- Craft knife
- Cutting board
- Steel-edged ruler
- Scissors
- Tooth picks
- Glue that is specifically suitable for cardstock projects
- Clothes pegs to clamp glued sections together to dry
- Paper clips to keep sections together and keep small glued pics in place
- Pencil and eraser to make marks that can be erased
- Empty ballpoint pen to score indentations for fold lines
- Invisible tape and double sided tape to use instead of glue for some projects
- Cardstock craft sheets in white or a solid color
- Acetate sheets if you want to photocopy the templates onto transparent sheets
- Gift ribbon and regular trimming ribbon
- A printer for the bonus templates in black and white
- A color printer for the free printable patterned paper sheets
- Containers or plastic bags for sorting items, themes and colors

THE CARDS

- The projects utilize the whole mix of cards one ends up with after the Holidays: the pretty, the so-so and the ugly. No fancy coordinated craft shop designs or expensive embellishments were used for this book. So just use whatever you have. The happy patchwork medley is exactly what provides the projects with their charm.

- If you have any cards lying in a box or drawer somewhere, you can start your crafting straight away. Ask friends, family and neighbors for theirs too. (They can white-out or black-out any private names and messages before they pass them on.)

- For bigger volume production you can ask for a collection box at Churches or religious centers, retirement homes and schools. Or put a little classified ad in your local newspaper and arrange for a pick up point. Local supermarkets and malls can get involved and have collection bins too. Also ask for used ribbon and wrapping paper.

- Why not begin a craft group and start making these ornaments, gifts and favors for the next season's holiday or charity markets? Likewise retirement centers, youth clubs, sports clubs and associations can form groups and make these crafts for their own fundraising efforts.

- And many of these projects are great for school craft classes to be given as gifts, used for school decorations or sold for school funds. Ask parents ahead of the holiday period to keep their cards.

- Folks love to browse craft fairs and shops for inexpensive "little something" gifts. Many of these projects provide just that.

- In the spirit of recycling, most of the projects were constructed entirely from used cards to limit the cost of purchased cardstock - but a few projects involved pictures cut from cards that were pasted onto a base made from cardstock. For craft classes the base card could even be cereal boxes or other packaging.

- To avoid confusion, I refer to the greeting cards in the projects as "used cards, Christmas cards, Holiday cards or greeting cards" and call any purchased card sheets "cardstock" throughout this book.

- Many of the small items are great to combine and they can be added to a nice mug or basket to make combo gifts and small gift hampers, or to give with flowers or seasonal greenery.

- Most of the projects in the series are very easy, but some are more time consuming (which you won't mind a bit because you'll find them so pretty). Maybe you should stick to the easy and very easy ones for volume production, and keep the more fiddly ones for your own satisfying makes. They are also suited to different time allocations.

- Feel free to add glitter or snow sparkle to some or all of the projects, while some are suited for fancy edges cut with decorative scissors.

THEMES

You may want to organize your stash of cards into image themes.

Examples would be:

- Trees, wreaths, houses, landscapes, doors and windows, flowers, musical instruments, reindeer, polar bears, penguins, domestic animals, sledges, Santa pics, angels, old fine art reproductions, peace doves, nativity scenes, snowflakes, holiday food, baubles, candles, and so on.

- Group cards with frame or border designs.

- And don't forget scenes from warm countries, cards with specialty themes like golf, or cards with all-over repeat designs. The latter are handy when a design needs to wrap around an object.

- You could sort them into color groups as an alternative – or into both themes and color groups.

- I particularly love a white-on white-look– or white plus color. The blank backs of used cards provide plenty of material for such items. Add some nice ribbon to finish an all-white item, or add a small picture.

- Those blank card backs are also ideal to repurpose as postcards by gluing pictures to them.

- Also set aside those cards that are good "word" candidates - cards that have prominent seasonal text. The text can be used as handles for baskets and seals or embellishments on all-white surfaces - or word strips for scrapbooking projects.

- Keep any gift tags with small images, as well as Holiday cards that have small pictures. They can be cut up for small embellishments on larger projects and for scrapbooking elements.

- Keep any wrapping paper off-cuts, as well as discarded envelopes.

- Assigning projects to cards is half the fun. I suggest you don't cut a card, before you have decided on a definite project for it.

- Have boxes, used envelopes and clear plastic bags ready for your word collections, small picture cut-outs and for bits of ribbon. Keep off-cuts too, as many projects are suitable for left over bits.

- Keep longer ribbon lengths separate. Use both gift ribbon and regular sewing ribbon.

- It is also optional to add some buttons and beads as trimming for some projects. They look super, don't cost much and a few go a long way.

THE TEMPLATES

The templates have lines and instructions on them and are at the back of the book. They are meant to be traced off or photocopied. For your convenience they are **also provided as downloads**, to print on to heavier cardstock. You can use the templates over and over again.

NOTE: The projects correspond to the template sheet numbers. The templates are not in logical order, as the templates were combined to best fit on the pages.

There are 45 template projects plus a few more that have no need for templates and have written instructions instead.

Because greeting cards vary so widely in format, I designed most of the templates to fit 5 x 7 inch (13 x 18 cm) cards which is a common size. The template size can be reduced or enlarged on computer or by photocopier - except for projects that need a specific final size.

Your bonus downloads include a second identical template collection which consists of printable templates that have no surface lines or instructions.

The bonus templates can be used with printable cardstock, which can be embellished with greeting card images instead of making the entire object from used greeting cards. Also use the blank templates to print onto your bonus Anni Arts pattern pages to construct base items that can be decorated with left-over bits of greeting cards.

Access the template collection and all the bonus free goodies as download links with your **best email address and receipt number** of this book at my Anni Arts website www.anniarts.com

Should you have any problems obtaining the templates and gifts, contact me via my Anni Arts contact page and I will send the link.

PROCEDURE

- Trace or photocopy the templates from the back of the book. Cut them out carefully to achieve a precise template to trace off. (The item will be easy to construct if the template has been correctly and carefully cut out.)

-An alternative is to photocopy each template on to clear acetate, so you can see the image on the greeting card and can move the template to best position it.

-Use a steel ruler and a craft knife to cut straight sections.

-Place the template onto the image of a used greeting card. Then trace around the template onto the used card with a pencil.

-Use an empty ballpoint pen to make a dotted dent on the greeting card at all points where you have to draw score lines to fold. Connect the dots by drawing a score line using a ruler for straight lines.

-TIP: Always gently fold scored lines in before folding out.

"Like" the Anni Arts Facebook page for blank craft templates used for the items above!

Download your **six bonus projects,** as well as the **pages of Anni Arts printable pattern paper** featuring gingham designs in Lime, Red, Xmas Green and Ochre. These can be used with the **second set of bonus downloadable blank templates** for paper crafts at http://www.anniarts.com. The templates in this book are also repeated as downloads. You need your **receipt number and email** address to access the download links.

*Note: **Library users will not be able to access the downloads,** because a receipt is needed, but you can still get the Facebook "Like" templates and freebies on the site.*

TABLE AND TREATS

Make table and food décor, as well as containers for yummy treats in jolly Seasonal style. Many of the table items can be made as collections to reuse for many years.

Cake Garland

Many, many cards depict Christmas Trees, so you are bound to have lots of them!

The following three projects make good use of cards depicting Christmas trees. You can also use any image and simply cut it into a Christmas tree shape. The first three projects have no templates, but full instructions are provided.

Keep the smallest tree images as toppers for the Cupcake Wraps (Project 5) the medium ones for the Cake Garland and Cake Topper decorations (Projects 1 and 2), and the largest tree images for the long Table Garland (Project 3).

A medley of tree styles results in a fun look. Or you can stick to images in either a traditional or contemporary style, or choose cute images for a children's cake. It all depends on what you have.

PROJECT 1- CAKE GARLAND

Very Easy

Full instructions follow. There are no templates for this project.

This cake is dressed for the occasion and the party.

The Cake Garland is best suited for cakes with hard icing. A moist cake with soft icing might cause the garland to become soggy. And remember to remove the garland before you cut the cake!

The Cake Garland also looks great combined with the Cake Topper trees in the next project and can also easily be adapted to make a crown for King Forest or the Xmas Fairy.

Tree images also make nice Christmas tree decorations - just punch a hole and add ribbon and perhaps some glitter and beads.

Make Cake Garland and Cake Topper sets to sell. Roll up each garland lightly, secure ends with a paper clip and place upright in a clear plastic bag. Place the loose tree toppers in the center of the rolled up garland. Tie the top of the plastic bag with pretty ribbon and add a tag or a word strip with a Holiday message. The sets can be expanded by adding coordinating Serviette Rings (Project), a Bottle Tie Tag, and reusable Place Cards (in the bonus downloads)

It is a good idea to make garlands in the popular cake tin circumference sizes. Remember to add a bit extra to the lengths for taping.

To store: Remove the ribbon (if used). Roll the garland up loosely and keep the ends secured with a paper clip. Put in a box or plastic container (with its ribbon, if used).

INSTRUCTIONS

- Use a pencil to lightly draw a stem at the base of the tree image below the "leaf line" of the tree (about half an inch/ 1 cm square).

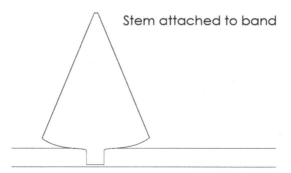

Stem attached to band

This stem - extending from the bottom of the image of the tree - is cut for each tree and will be glued to a band that goes around the cake.
If the trees will be taller than the cake (as on the photo), you could use two images back-to-back. If the cake is taller than the garland that runs around it, then only single images are required.

For the band around the cake:
- Measure the circumference of the cake.
- Cut a strip of card stock about an inch (2.5 cm) wide and about half an inch (1 cm) longer than the measurement of the circumference.
- Position the tree images along the band.
- Keep them tightly spaced to make the cake garland. They can even slightly overlap.
- Glue each tree to the base via the stem extension, keeping the half inch (1 cm) extra length free at the end of the band.
- Put a piece of double-sided tape on that extra section and close the band once it is around the cake.
- This band can be covered with a ribbon or the strip of cardstock can be embellished with punched holes, punched shapes or small pics.

To make double-sided trees:
- Cut out the shape and stem extension of the larger of two tree images.
- Place it face-down on the image of a card with a smaller tree, lining up the top of the "pyramid" tree shapes.
- Trace around the shape of the larger tree, as well as its stem. The second tree will thus conform to the overall shape of the larger one.
- Turn them face-out with the blank sides together and glue the two trees together. You can use a clothes pin to keep them in position.
- If you don't want to make double-sided images, you can make the blank side more interesting by adding a little cut-out of a smaller tree or some other little image, words or text onto the blank side of single tree images.

PROJECT 2 - CAKE TOPPERS

Very Easy

Instructions are barely needed – just add cake!

*Make these with toothpicks and images of trees.
Turn any cake or slice into a festive pastry or Holiday dessert!*

If the tree image has a natural stem, or if the tree is in a planter or pot, those can be retained if you wish. Otherwise the tree images can be trimmed at the base of the tree line, as the toothpick forms a stem for each tree.

Tape the toothpick to the back of the image. The toothpick needs to extend at least an inch (2.5 cm) beyond the base of the tree.

If you choose, these can be made with double-sided images so that they can be viewed from any side. Double-sided cake toppers also serve to hide the toothpick which gets inserted into the icing.

For double-sided toppers, follow the same procedure for making the back-to-back images for the Cake Garland, but do not cut a stem. It helps to clamp the two pictures together with a clothespin or paper clip so they stay together while the glue dries.

You can also add a cut-out of a smaller tree or some other small image, word or text to the blank back of a single image if you wish. Choose to make one large Cake Topper tree or a whole little forest!

And small images of trees make nice lapel pins for parties. Tape a safety pin to the back. You can add a word strip for extra flair or personalize it with a name.

PROJECT 3 - TABLE GARLAND

Very Easy

Full instructions follow. There are no templates for this project.

This meandering zigzag garland will look equally good on a table, mantle, above a fireplace, or on a shelf. Make it as long as you please.

Use the largest images from your tree stash for this visually pleasing project. As before, a mix of images will make a cheerful project, but a color coordinated, style or themed garland will also be lovely.

For use on a table, the garland must be attractive to view from all sides. I suggest the double- sided picture treatment as described for the Cake Garland and Cake Toppers, but without stem or toothpick.

For a mantle or shelf the garland can be comprised of one-sided images.

To make the garland sturdier, do not extend a stem to paste on a band, but rather use the wide base of the tree as a surface to glue to a zigzag base strip.

The Table Garland will also make a nice window or wall frieze. And you can keep on adding to it year by year until it can stretch across an entire wall – or around a room!

Note: Double-sided images will make the unit heavier, so use thick cardstock for the zigzag base to prevent the trees from pulling the garland over.

INSTRUCTIONS

- Cut the images along their outlines and along the base of the triangular tree shape.

- Measure the width of the base of the widest image.
This is the width that each zigzag section of the base of the garland will be.

- Count how many images you have to add to the band. This amount multiplied with the width of the widest tree gives you the length of the strip for the base of the garland.

- Cut a base strip from sturdy craft cardstock. Make it at least two inches (5cm) tall.

- The taller the trees, the taller (and thicker) the cardstock strip must be to form a sturdy base that won't topple. If you need a base that is longer than the length of your card-stock, glue sections of base together to achieve the desired length.

- Use a ruler to divide the length of the base strip into sections to the measurement of the widest tree and mark with pencil at each measured unit.
If your widest image is 2 1/2" (5cm) wide, then that is the width each of the zigzag sections will be. If you have 20 tree images, the length of the strip will be 20 times the widest measurement, thus 50 inches or 100 cm.

- Use an empty ball point pen and set square to score a straight line down the base strip at each division mark you made in pencil.

- Fold this score mark back.

- Repeat for the second score mark, but fold the scored line forwards.

- Repeat the process, alternating the forward and backward folds to form the concertina zigzag sections.

- Now glue the trees to the base – one tree to a zigzag section – by applying glue to about half an inch (1 cm) to the base of the tree and gluing to the strip.

- If you are working with double-sided images, leave about half an inch (1 cm) free of glue at the base of the trees when you glue the rest of the images together.
When you're ready to glue the image to the base strip, apply glue to this area between the two images and straddle the base strip when you glue the unit to it.

- Continue to glue the images to the base strip until you have used all your images.

The garland folds up neatly concertina style on the score lines of the zigzag sections.

PROJECT 4 - CANDY TRAY

Easy

Template is on Sheet 20

Party snacks at various year-end gatherings and kid's Christmas parties are the perfect occasions to put these little snack trays to use.

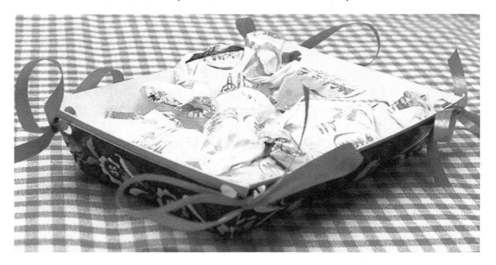

Use only wrapped candy and chocolates, as greeting cards are not made for direct contact with food. Using food that will stain and mark the tray, will also make it unfit for future reuse. You can also line the inside with wax paper or a paper serviette cut to size.

Make use of snippets of left-over ribbon for the corner tags – achieve a nice mismatched look by using ribbons that are not the same. Ribbon can be gift wrap or sewing ribbons. The image can also be on the inside of the tray.

PROJECT 5 - CUPCAKE WRAPPER

Easy

Template is on Sheet 31

Cupcakes in pretty and festive wrappers are perfect stand-ins for a traditional Holiday or Christmas cake – and they will please everyone.

Two cards are needed for a single wrapper - the back and front will have different pictures. They can also both be cut from the same card if it has an all-over design, or from a picture unit and a blank unit.

Use any small picture as a topper, or cut a star from the template on Sheet 20. Small tree images or the small dove or angel pic sizes can also be used as cupcake toppers.

Display these on an elevated or tiered cake stand for a gorgeous display. Dress the cupcakes with silver balls, chocolate sprinkles or vermicelli to match the wrappers.

Make sure cupcakes are in baking paper cups before placing in the wrappers, as greeting cards are not manufactured to be in direct contact with food.

Cupcake Wrappers also make sweet gift containers for gloves, socks, baby clothing or other small items like a face cloth, tea lights and cupcake soaps.

Sell in sets as ready items, together with little toppers on toothpicks. Make lots!

PROJECT 6 - TRUFFLE BOX

Easy

Template is on Sheet 2

The little truffle box is ideal for a few deluxe chocolate truffles.

It is an ideal container with real gift "presence" for small gifts that would otherwise look insignificant in tiny packaging.

Two sides are cut from one card, so the completed box has a combination of two images. The two images can be related in theme or color.

Glue the two sections together and tape the bottom to make it secure. Slip the sections with punch holes through the two sections with slots. Weave ribbon through the slots and tie with a bow. Add a tag to finish the look.

PROJECT 7 - TEA BOX AND ENVELOPES

Easy

Template is on Sheets 17 and 18

The tea box fits a stack of tea bags in pretty tea bag envelopes.
It makes a cute and practical gift or favor.

Two sides are cut from a single landscape card, so the four sides of the box will be made up of two wraparound images. The images can be themed or a random mix.

The lid can be cut from the blank card back and have a square topper glued to it, or it can be cut from a complete image.

The tea bag envelopes can be cut from leftover wrapping paper too. Fill each envelope with a teabag. The actual tea tag can also be topped with a small image. The bonus printable pattern sheets included in the template download also make nice envelopes. Top with squares cut from Holiday cards.

Fill the box with as many tea bag envelopes as fit inside the box.
Tea bag envelopes cut from card will be thicker than those cut from paper, so the amount of teabag envelopes that fit in the box will depend on the material used.

PROJECT 8 - CHOCOLATE WRAPPERS

Easy

Template is on Sheet 6

Chocolates are indispensable at Christmas time, so dress them for the feast.

Keep several ready as quick gifts for co-workers, neighbors and teachers. Even a small snack bar is a nice little gift of appreciation when thoughtfully wrapped.

Wrapped chocolates make nice "little something" gifts for hostesses and make handy table favors for guests too. They are a great addition to those Christmas luncheons at retirement centers and clubs. Personalize and place one at each place setting. They can even be used instead of place cards.

A card wrapper does not have to fit the chocolate exactly, as it actually forms a sleeve that is perfect for decorating.

The first example *(left on the photo opposite)* was made from white card backing, with an additional narrower wrap cut from a picture card. A snippet of ribbon and a star picture add further decorations. You can add a nice tag too.

The second example *(right on the photo opposite)* has a wrapper cut from leftover wrapping paper, and is embellished with a Holiday card and bow.

For large bars like Swiss *Lindt* slabs, greeting card fronts or shaped pictures can be applied as toppers after the item has been wrapped in regular wrapping paper or brown Kraft paper. Brown Kraft paper looks super when dressed up with lots of red.

You can also use one of the bonus printable gingham pattern sheets included in the template downloads. The lime paper has a fresh look and coordinates with any color.

Several wrap layers can be added. Make each strip narrower than the previous one. The layering idea can be applied to any size slab. Incorporate lace, braids and ribbon.

Score the edges of very thick cardstock where the card folds around to the back to prevent the card from cracking.

Note: A second, larger chocolate wrapper template for a European 100g chocolate slab is included in the bonus downloads. The size was too large to fit within the printable margins of this book.

PROJECT 9 - COOKIES FOR SANTA PLATE

Very Easy

Template is on Sheet 25

This is a perfect project for using up an odd selection of cards.

Position the star template so that an image is nicely in the center of the star.
The example has 12 stars arranged around a plate with a circumference of 28 inches (70 cm). You can keep them in place with a paper clip until you are happy with the spacing. Then glue each one into place.

Line the plate with a paper serviette or wax paper before adding the cookies, so it will be durable and ready for Santa for many years.

Also consider Christmas trees, angels or peace doves as images for the Cookie Plate. Or combine several for a mixed theme.

This also makes an easy wreath - just cut the center from a paper plate before arranging and gluing the stars into place on the rim.

PROJECT 10 - SERVIETTE RINGS

Very Easy

Template is on Sheet 10

Serviette rings made from Holiday cards look great with paper or textile serviettes.

Cut strips from pictures, or from the blank card backs. Add additional cut-out pictures and/ or narrow word strips to the serviette rings. Choose childlike themes for the children's table and more sophisticated ones for the grownups. You can also cut decorative edges or add glitter to the edges.

An alternative type of serviette ring can be made by shape-cutting a picture, taping it to ribbon, and tying the ribbon around the serviette. Smart ribbon in velvet or lace will look lovely around cloth or embroidered serviettes.

The small versions of the star, the dove or the angel images can also be used to cut a silhouette shape from any image.

Get a coordinating reusable place card template in the bonus downloads.

BOXES AND LITTLE GIFTS

*Packaging and tags for little gifts, books and luggage,
plus small items that make great favors and stocking stuffers.*

PROJECT 11- LIDDED GIFT BOX

Easy

Template is on Sheets 23 and 25

Purchased cardstock was used for the base of the box and Red Robin pictures where cut for the sides, lid and seal and then glued to the sides and top of the lid. Use any themed pictures or a mix of pictorial matter.

The seal is optional and is only glued in place once the gift is in the box.

Make sure that both the sides and the bottom are glued very well. Additionally, tape the bottom to make sure a heavy item won't drop out. A ribbon tied around the box - when the lid is on - will keep all together in a pretty and secure way too.

PROJECT 12 - SMALL GIFT BOX

Easy

Template is on Sheet 15

This handy gift box is an all-purpose container for candy and small gifts.

It was constructed from purchased cardstock first. Pictures from Holiday cards were cut to size and then glued to the top and sides of the box. The box can also be cut entirely from cards. Whimsical images of reindeer were used for this project and it was sealed with a word strip. The template can be enlarged to make a bigger box.

PROJECT 13 - POCKET TISSUE PACK

Easy

Template is on Sheet 11 and 38

Holiday time is sneeze time and most everyone can use an extra packet of handy pocket tissues. Make lots of these quick and handy gift items. There is also a template for a larger European pocket tissue packet (Sheet 38.

PROJECT 14 - TAGS

Very Easy

Templates are on Sheets 1, 2, 3, 4, 7, 10 and 11

A few shaped tags are included as extras in the template section

GIFT TAGS

Never run out of gift tags again. If you do only one recycling project, let it be this one!

You can get more than one from a single card depending on the type of image on the card. Beautiful pictorial areas of used cards will yield many gift tags and can be coordinated with plain or patterned wrapping paper.

BOOKMARK

Bookmarks are perfect little gifts for booklovers. For this project, you can use card off-cuts and even get a few out of one card if the picture has an all-over design. Use the template as a size guide only. Finish with a tail of ribbon and maybe a bead too.

A bookmark is a nice little gift to send with a greeting card and it is, of course, perfect to add to a book gift. It can be a gift tag that becomes a useful bookmark later.

LUGGAGE TAG

With so many people traveling over the holiday period, luggage tags are handy items to have on hand. Tie to luggage pieces, kid's rucksacks and toys too.

If you know the address of the recipient, you can even laminate the tag after sliding the address into the slot to make it more durable.

PROJECT 15 - PILLOW PACK

Easy

Template is on Sheet 1

Pillow packs are a snap to make and assemble.

This one makes a sturdy pack for a variety of small gifts.

Score the curved lines of the end flaps carefully and well. Use an empty ballpoint pen to score the lines. Then fold and glue the side. Fold the curved flaps in to close. It is optional to tape the closed flaps to seal the ends.

Enlarge the template on a copier and use with purchased cardstock if you want to make a larger package from cardstock. And reduce the template size if you want to make the pack from a smaller greeting card.

It can also be a white pack with added ribbon and picture embellishments.

PROJECT 16 - WEDGE BOXES

Easy

Templates are on Sheets 35, 36 and 37

These pretty containers are lovely boxes for cake and candy treats or small gifts.

Included are three templates for large and small upright boxes, plus a flat "cake slice box". The templates are in two units for the larger two, in order to use two card fronts.

They also make nice Christmas tree decorations if you punch holes in the upright boxes and thread with ribbon. These boxes make nice Advent boxes too.

An acetate template allows you to find the best picture view. Position the acetate template to find a pleasant part of the picture on at least one prominent side.

The flat wedge-shaped "cake slice box" (Sheet 37) can be filled with favors or candy. It can also be filled with an actual wedge-shaped slice of fruit cake or other type of festive cake or bread. Wrap each slice in food safe plastic first.

A super way to use the cake slice box is to make many and actually arrange them in a circle as a sliced "cake". This can take the place of a real Christmas cake. Decorate with cake toppers as in Project 2. These are great take-home favors for guests or party goers. Make the cake circle as large as is needed, or stack a smaller circle (or more) on a big one to make a tiered cake. This option will use up a lot of cards.

PROJECT 17- BASKET

Easy

Template is on Sheets 5 and 26

The basket is great for cookies, sweets, or a jar of preserves wrapped in a serviette.

You can construct this basket entirely from four used cards, or cut the basket from purchased cardstock as a single item to decorate with greeting card pictures.

A collection of sledge images were used with one image glued to each side. A long strip of Holiday text was used as a handle. Add a tag and you have a lovely gift pack. The images can be themed or a random selection.

It can also function as a container for a collection of small items. Make mini gift baskets as personal gifts or to sell.

Examples for gift baskets are: A bath basket with soap, a wash cloth and fizz ball; a baking or cooking basket with spices and herbs; a hot chocolate basket with cocoa, sprinkles and marshmallows; or a food basket with nuts, cookies, salty snacks or chocolates. Put edibles in food safe plastic bags first.

Note: Secure the bottom, seams and handle very well with tape if you plan to put a heavy item in the basket. The handles can also be stapled on.

PROJECT 18 - GOLF BALL BOX

Easy

Template is on Sheet 3

This little gift box is perfectly sized to take a golf ball.

The golf ball box makes a super stocking filler and you can put it to very good use! Many Holiday cards have golfing themes, but any random image will do. An all-over pattern will work well, as the box is so small. The box can also be made from cardstock.

Make lots of them. It's a great gift from kids to dad or grandpa and super to sell as stocking stuffers! Display a sample with a golf ball in it.

It can be combined with other small items in a mug or basket to make a little gift hamper. A special artisan truffle is another item that is perfect for the little box – as is a piece of jewelry or small charms. Some coffee capsules will also fit in the box.

PROJECT 19 - SEWING KIT

Easy

Template is on Sheet 9

Holiday travelers are bound to need an emergency sewing kit.

Cut a card just smaller than the back of the sewing kit box. Wind thread in different colors around it in separate sections and in good lengths. Tape a needle, safety pins and some white shirt buttons to the card. A thread cutter or tiny pair of scissors can also be included, but be mindful of airline specifications regarding sharp implements.

PROJECT 20 - FESTIVE MATCHBOX

Very Easy

This matchbox in festive gear is ready for lighting the Holiday candles.

Measure the top of any matchbox you want to embellish, and cut a picture to fit. Glue to the top of the matchbox. It pairs nicely with the candle gift in Project 23.

PACKETS AND POCKETS

Sweet smelling sachets, heart packets, sleeves and pockets for little gifts

Gift Card Envelope, Heart Sachet and Candle Sleeve

PROJECT 21- HEART SACHET

Very Easy

Template is on Sheet 8

Put some dried lavender, Rose petals, citrus peel and spices, or other potpourri in this heart sachet. Seal the packet with double-sided tape on the inside of the heart, so that no dried potpourri falls out. *(Center front on photo)*

This project uses the picture front, as well as the plain back of the card in one unit. The front has flaps that fold back and are glued to the back of the heart. It can also be cut from two image units. The template includes both options.

You can use a pin to prick some tiny holes in the card so that the fragrance can escape. The nicest is to prick the holes at even intervals along the edge of the heart – about 1/4 inch (1/2 a cm) in from the edge. Or you can follow the outlines of the picture on the heart.

Punch two holes at the top and tie a ribbon so it can be hooked over a coat hanger or hang from the handle of a cupboard or drawer. Without ribbon it can be placed in a drawer or linen cupboard.

You can also make twenty-four numbered hearts for Advent, and string them across a wall. Or make seven for the week before Christmas as countdown favors.

PROJECT 22 - GIFT CARD ENVELOPE

Easy

Template is on Sheet 31

A gift card envelope makes a nice presentation for an otherwise boring looking present. A gift card unfortunately doesn't look like much regardless of the money value of the card *(Top left on photo opposite)*. They are very popular gift items - especially for late gifts and desperate gift givers. So make lots of these handy little envelopes.

PROJECT 23 - CANDLE SLEEVE

Very Easy

Template is on Sheet 13

There can never be too many candles at Christmas and the candle sleeve provides a nice gift presentation. *(Right on photo opposite)*. Choose a card to wrap around two candles. The picture front of a landscape card is easily wide enough. Secure at the back with tape. The wrapper can also be white with various decorations added.

This is a nice project for using strips of cards and picture toppers in layers. Add additional ribbon, word strips and tags. You can start the layers with used gift wrap too. This makes a super hostess gift when paired with the decorated match box (Project 20).

Note: Some cards crack when they are folded, so it is best to make a sleeve by scoring a line straight down the wrapper on both sides at the point where the card wraps to the back of the candles.

Scent Sachet and Tie Tag

PROJECT 24 - SCENT SACHET

Easy

Template is on Sheet 33

This scent sachet (*Topmost on photo*) is constructed from a single landscape card. The hanging tag is cut from the back of the card. The punched hole fits a coat hanger with a metal hook. Alternatively, the sachet can be hooked over a coat hanger, drawer pull or hook by a ribbon loop.

Punched holes as described in Project 21 are a nice way to finish the sachet, as well as being a practical mechanism for the fragrance to escape.

If you are making one for a laundry cupboard, you can omit the hanging tag. It is a good idea to tape over the opening so that the potpourri doesn't fall out.

Make lots for lovely quick and easy gifts.

PROJECT 25 - TIE TAG

Very Easy

Template is on Sheet 13

This tag will stay with its parcel! The size is ideal for wrapped soap boxes and other smallish gifts. It is very prominent on the gift, so choose nice sections of picture cards for this project and then add coordinating ribbon. *(Bottom on photo opposite.)*

The tie tag is easy to adapt as a tie label around a festive jar. Add a round picture to the jar lid, plus a tag for extra flair. Get the tie tag for a wine bottle as bonus template.

PROJECT 26 - GIFT CARD STOCKING

Easy

Template is on Sheet 4

This stocking gives some nice bulk to a gift card. This is especially true for children who prefer gifts with a nice "thud value"! When you glue the stocking front to its back, leave an unglued pocket the size of a credit card for inserting a gift card. Add a ribbon and hang in the tree, or over a door or cupboard handle. It is advisable to keep the tip of the gift card peeping out so that it is clearly visible.

Dimensional Card, Bag Topper and Mini Gift Bag

PROJECT 27 - BAG TOPPER

Easy

Paper bags make handy gift containers for things like cookies, candy, chocolates and small items that are difficult to wrap. A bag topper forms a nice seal, and one cut from a Christmas card is super quick to make to add to a purchased bag. *(Right on photo)*

The fold of the bag topper can be on the natural fold of a landscape card so that the card is stapled to a paper bag in its entirety. This would be suitable for a large paper bag. It can also be trimmed to a narrower or shorter size. The back of the topper will then be blank. Decorate with bits and bobs.

Alternatively, the image side can be used to form both the front and the back of the topper with the fold running width-wise through the middle of the image. An all-over repeat design is best for this option.

PROJECT 28 - MINI GIFT BAG

Easy

Template is on Sheet 7

The itty bitty mini bag is a practical container for a teensy gift like a piece of jewelry, a charm, lip balm, a flash drive or a golf divot or tee. It uses the picture side of a card, but can also be made as an all-white gift bag. *(Bottom right on photo)*.It can be decorated with words or small pictures and can be sealed with a picture or word strip. The edge can be cut with decorative scissors. Punch holes for an optional ribbon tie or handles.

PROJECT 29 - REUSABLE DIMENSIONAL CARD

Easy

It is easy to make a dimensional card if you happen to have more than one of the same greeting card. Cut individual pictures from the second card and glue them to the base card with little foam squares made for dimensional card making. If you have three of the same cards you can build up images in three layers

To make the card reusable, cut an insert from plain paper that is slightly smaller than the card itself. Write – or type – a message on the insert and slip into the card or tie with a ribbon through the middle fold. You can type a message in small text on the inset and ask the recipient to reuse and recycle the card by adding a new insert. You can also cut slits on the inside to keep a message notelet in place. This gets replaced with a new notelet when the card goes to a next recipient.

PROJECT 30 - WOVEN HEART POCKET

Tricky

Template is on Sheet 17

When this classic Danish heart is complete, it must form a pocket.

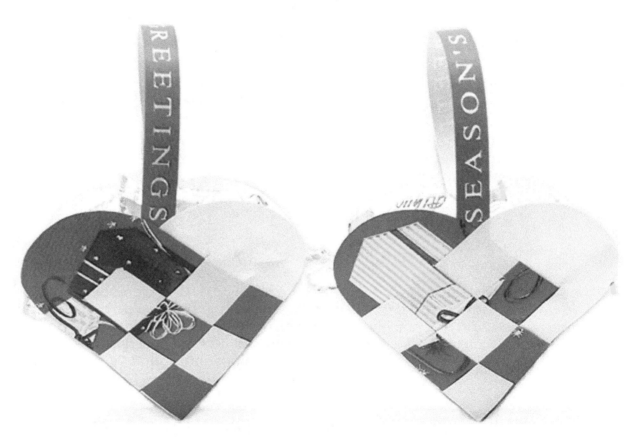

The hearts are often incorrectly depicted as flat decorations in many craft books. You can fill it with candy or a heart shaped ginger cookie.

The construction method is not easy to describe, but comprehensive step-by-step instructions with illustrated diagrams are provided. Try it out on spare paper first to get the hang of it!

You need two folded units. They need to have a nice color contrast to form the well-known woven square pattern. Cutting them from a folded card provides a white side, so make sure the image side of the card does not contain a lot of white to achieve the desired contrast. An image with lots of red will look like the traditional hearts.

The left and right images on the photo are the same item from the front and the back.

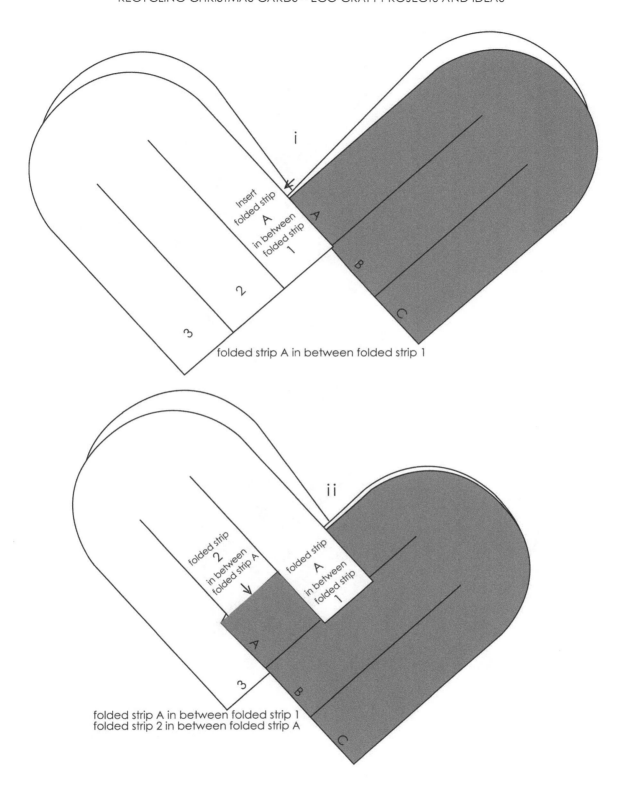

i

Insert folded strip A in between folded strip 1

folded strip A in between folded strip 1

ii

folded strip 2 in between folded strip A

folded strip A in between folded strip 1

folded strip A in between folded strip 1
folded strip 2 in between folded strip A

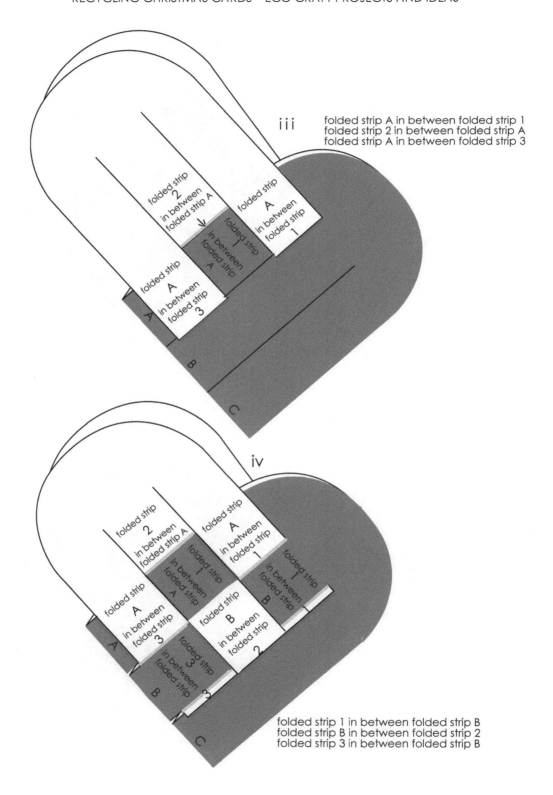

iii

folded strip A in between folded strip 1
folded strip 2 in between folded strip A
folded strip A in between folded strip 3

iv

folded strip 1 in between folded strip B
folded strip B in between folded strip 2
folded strip 3 in between folded strip B

v

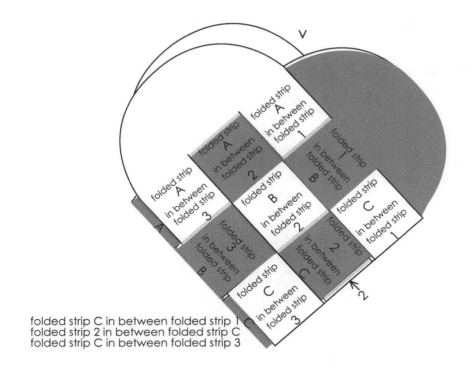

folded strip C in between folded strip 1
folded strip 2 in between folded strip C
folded strip C in between folded strip 3

vi
pocket

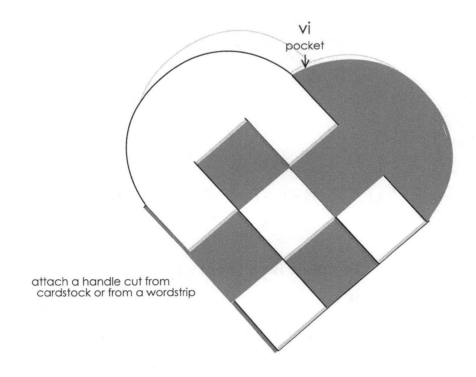

attach a handle cut from
cardstock or from a wordstrip

DECORATIONS AND ORNAMENTS

Baubles, stars, little houses and trees give used Holiday cards a new decorative life.

PROJECT 31- BALL ORNAMENT

Takes Time

Template is on Sheet 20

This project is ideal for using up much of your card stash in one go.

It's the type of project you can repeat year after year for a collection of stylish and long lasting decorations. The sample was made from pictures of round wreaths, but this works with snippets of any pics. Bits of off-cuts that have no clear image are also fine.

Choose random colors or select cards in a specific color scheme. The ball also looks very classy as an all-white snow ball. Add velvet or patterned ribbon as contrast.

INSTRUCTIONS:

The instructions actually make it sound more complex than it is, so don't be put off from trying to make this lovely item.

-The template has a triangle in a circle. You need 20 circles.
Trace the circular shape, plus lines for the triangle onto the card. The triangle needs to be scored thoroughly to make folding easy. Use a ruler to draw the score lines of the triangle. Fold the circle sections that fall outside of the triangle forwards.
- Arrange the triangle/circles in two heaps of five and one heap of ten units. The units of five form the top and bottom domes and the unit of ten forms the middle band.
- For each dome: apply glue to the two side flaps of the first circle/ triangle unit.
- Glue a circle/ triangle unit to each side flap. You have now used three units.
- Then glue a unit to each of the side flaps of the outer two and lastly glue the fifth and first units together to form a dome.
The first photo shows the two domes and the middle band, and the second photo shows the bottom dome attached to the middle band without the top dome.
- Leave a little gap in the top dome to insert a ribbon to hang the ornament.
 -For the middle band: arrange the ten circle/triangles in a row. Alternate the down-pointing triangles with up- pointing triangles. Glue the flaps together. Keep on adding the other seven units in this way to form the band.
- Then glue together the first and last units to close the band into a circle.
 - Glue the band to the top dome via the top flap of each triangle on the band which has its point pointing down.
- Now do the same by gluing the bottom dome to flaps of the remaining triangles which have their points pointing up.
- This results in a nice ball. Add ribbon to finish.

PROJECT 32 - CONE ICICLES

Very Easy

Template is on Sheet 32

There are two template sizes for these icicle tree decorations. The larger one fits a 5" x 7" card and the smaller is for a 4" x 6" card or postcard.

The picture side, as well as the white backing of a greeting card, make nice icicles. Use cut-out pics on all-white cones. Punch holes, and add ribbon, word strips or tags as needed. Fill with small sweets, candy canes, lollipops, or rolled-up money notes and hang in the Christmas tree. They look nice as an icicle row in a window too. Another alternative is to make them from clear acetate, with greeting card embellishments.

This project can also be adapted for Advent: Add the template numbers to 24 icicles. They can be cut from the very last page without damaging the book too much.

PROJECT 33 - ZIGZAG BORDER

Very Easy

Template is on Sheet 19

A festive zigzag border is just the thing to edge a shelf for the Holiday season.

This is an ideal project to use up bits and bobs, as it is not necessary to have clearly recognizable images in the triangles. It is the impression of the whole that counts. Make it as long as is needed.

You can also add to it year by year until you can string it around a room! Paper fasteners were used to string the triangles together, but the project will work just as well if the triangles are strung together with ribbon as for the Bunting in Project 50.

Style the border with Holiday crockery on a dresser or shelf to complete the festive look.

(Ceramic mugs, plate and tile in the photo are Anni Arts designs that have been licensed by a manufacturer. Licensing info on www.anniarts.com)

And get the original Happy Reindeer and Swedish Jul printables on Anni Arts Crafts
www.anniartscrafts.com

PROJECT 34 - 3D STAR

Tricky

Template is on Sheet 9

The star is a little bit tricky on the final stages, but is oh so worth it!

The units of the star made for this project are color coordinated with blue backgrounds and themed with childlike subject matter. A patchwork medley of different card themes and colors will look just as pleasing. The star can also be entirely white. Punch holes or shapes before constructing it, but add glitter after constructing it.

Two construction methods are described.

Note that you can also make a one-sided star to hang against a cupboard or a wall – the construction is certainly easier than the two-sided version and it will look just as nice!

INSTRUCTIONS

Cut five image units and five white units – or ten image units if you want images on both sides of the star. You can also cut all ten units from white card backs. Score the center line of each star point – both front and back units – and fold so that each star point is slightly raised. A good contact glue made for cardstock crafts is essential.

There are two different assembly methods described below.

Method 1: Glue the front and back of each point unit together, and then proceeded to glue the units together in threes and twos. Then glue the three point unit and the two point unit to each other as in the picture above. The last step is quite fiddly to glue.

Method 2: Glue 5 units together for the top and 5 units for the bottom after scoring and folding the center line slightly. Note that the 5 units cannot lie flat when glued – they must be folded and be raised slightly on the center line. Glue the flaps of the front unit of five to the back unit of five. It is quite easy until the flaps of the last back and front have to be glued. Pressing the two glue surfaces together on the flaps is a tad tricky.

PROJECT 35 - MINIATURE HOUSES

Easy

Templates are on Sheets 13 and 26

*Those lovely pictures of snow-covered houses are perfect for these two projects, but the house shapes can also be cut from any other images –just add window apertures.
Or cut windows in an all-white snowy house!*

TEA-LIGHT HOUSES

The tea-light house template has no roof because it contains an electric tea candle.

Do not place roofs on the houses - even with electric candles - as heat can collect under the paper. And never use live-flame candles with this project!

Choose house images from which it is possible to cut out the window squares. These look gorgeous when the candle inside the house makes the light glow in the little windows. And they are all the better at night time.

Use a single card image to wrap around two sides of a house and glue that to another two-sided unit. So a gable and non-gable side forms a single unit.

PLAY HOUSES

The village house versions have snow roofs cut from white card backs. They make nice play houses and are thus ideal for play schools to use over the Holiday period.

The houses also make lovely mantle scenes, shelf decorations or hanging tree decorations. Punch a hole through the folded roof before attaching it to the house and add ribbon to hang. Add little people, cars and trees to complete a village scene.

And for Advent they can get roof numbers and hide candy!

PROJECT 36 - ROUND BAUBLES

Tricky

Template is on Sheet 12

These bauble decorations can be plain or very lavish. Dress them up or down.

This project is tricky if attempted by just one person. Ideally you need one person to tie the knots in the ribbon, while another keeps the strips lightly pushed into a ball shape. With two people working together it is actually a super easy project.

It is a very economical project, as many strips can be cut from a single card. At least one complete decoration can be made from a card front. Each ball needs four strips.

The strips are too narrow to show a recognizable picture and thus do not need to be cut from the same pictorial matter, but you might want to have a color theme for each bauble. Non-descript off-cuts from other projects are perfect for this project, as the charm lies in the shape of the object.

All-white decorations from the card backs combined with ribbon, beads or pictures are pretty too. White balls with red and white gingham have a distinct Scandinavian look.

The baubles can be decorated further with beads, buttons and bits of ribbon. Tiny pics can also be glued to one or more strips. Beads are a good way to add weight to the finished decoration. Leave enough length of ribbon at the bottom and top for the beads. Feathers or butterflies are also nice additions – as are orphaned earrings!

Do not try to use this template on very stiff card, as the card strips will bend and crack instead of forming a ball shape. Once it has formed a fold like that, it will not curve smoothly for the ball shape!

- First cut out the four strips.
- Punch holes through all the circles. Do this one by one and place the hole nicely in the center of the circle.
- Lay the four strips in a stack with the center hole of each on top of the one below.
- Thread the start of a ribbon through the center leaving a tail.
- Tie a loose knot in this tail under the center to keep the threaded centers from slipping out. (The knot must be bigger than the hole.) Wide ribbon will be easier to thread if you roll the point and wrap it in some tape – much like a shoelace.
- Now fold the two innermost strips up and thread the ribbon through their two combined holes at the top. It is important to thread the strips in the sequence that they lie. Otherwise the finished shape will not form a nice ball.
- Make sure that the knot at the bottom end does not slip through the circles.
- Fold the next two strips up and thread through the top two holes.
- Fold the last strip up and thread through the top two holes.
- You will now have a decoration with a long oblong shape.
- Carefully press the strips down from the top to make a ball shape. Card cracks easily and will make a deep fold on the crack, so proceed lightly!
- When the shape is a pleasing ball, make another knot just above all the threaded top circles to keep the shape under tension.
- You can tie a bow at the top and bottom ends (leave a long enough tail at the bottom if you intend doing this). Tie a loop above the knot from which to hang the decoration if you do not add a bow. Tie the loop to the bow if you do make a bow.
- The important thing is to have a knot top and bottom that will not slip through the holes. The knots at the top and bottom of the strips are what keep the bauble under tension to form the ball shape. An alternative would be to make the ball with florist wire.

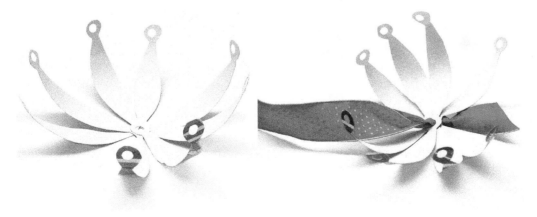

PROJECT 37 - CIRCLE STRINGS

Very Easy

Template is on Sheet 29

This project is great for using up odd cards. Make one or many strings!

The example was made from snowflake images, but any images will do. Use different sizes for variety and space the circles as you please.

A few strands will look great in a window and many strands can make a door curtain. The strand can also be strung horizontally to string around a room or table edge.

Use twine, wool or ribbon as string. The circles are best attached with double-sided tape if ribbon is used, and with regular tape for wool or twine.

PROJECT 38 - TRIANGLE TREE DECORATION

Very Easy

Template is on Sheet 19

The triangle tree can be a standing decoration or a hanging ornament.

If it is constructed from a whole card, there will be two picture sides and one blank side on the triangle (an all-over design works best). Decorate the blank side with pics or elements.

For a hanging ornament, punch holes before assembling the tree. The three sides can also be cut separately from three pictures so that each picture can be placed in the best position. The template allows for either option.

Pyramid Favor, Little Tree Ornament and Triangle Tag

PROJECT 39- LITTLE TREE ORNAMENT

Easy

Template is on Sheet 34

The 3D table decoration is quickly assembled by slotting the two tree-shaped units together and opening the tree so it can stand on its base on a table, mantle or a shelf. *(Top right on photo)*

The two units should be cut from two picture fronts or two white cards for a white tree which you can decorate with small pictures or words.

It makes a perfect little card plus gift item! It only requires the recipient to slot the two halves together for an instant decoration.

The little tree can also be turned into a Christmas tree decoration by punching holes in the top of each segment and inserting a ribbon loop.

PROJECT 40 - PYRAMID FAVOR

Easy

Template is on Sheet 14

A pretty pyramid-shaped container makes a nice table favor.

It is perfect to contain an item like a piece of jewelry, a tree decoration, a small bauble, an artisan chocolate in a paper cup or a meringue confection on a wax paper lining. *(Left on photo opposite).*

It can be cut entirely from a single greeting card with three sides falling on the image side and one side falling on the blank back of the card. Decorate the blank side with a picture or small elements.

The pyramid also makes a nice tree decoration - with or without a little something inside.

You can also use the triangles as gift tags by cutting them loose from the base. See the example on the plate and below. A tag template is included on Sheet 14.

Food for thought – start crafting with used cards straight away!

MEMORIES AND DÉCOR

Scrapbook stockings and pages make great Holiday décor for walls or coffee tables and posters deck the walls for the season!

Make pages for albums or to frame them for scrapbook walls! Bring albums and/or framed pics out for the Holidays. And add some every year for a record of Christmases past.

The scrapbook projects remind one of the true origins of scrapbooking when Christmas and greeting cards were routinely used to make scrap pages. Scrapbook items and tags are a super way to use all kinds of bits and pieces. Many of the projects in this book can get the scrapbook treatment, so adapt them using the ideas in this chapter.

Frame complete pages, as well as the card and postcard examples as Christmas memories to display during the season. And Holiday Scrapbooks make for great conversation pieces. Start assembling a scrapbook to display as a coffee table book over the Holidays.

The examples include a 6"x 6" card, an 8"x 8" page, a 6"x 4" postcard, two stockings and a few extra scrap tags. The tags can be used as gift tags or tree decorations and can be added to other decorations like the baubles, bunting and many more. Tags can be made from the tag templates. The card and postcard are also perfect photo gifts to post in a flat envelope.

In general, choose cards that have elements like a frame, border design, wreaths, words and frames.

Add small accent pics, pretty borders, blank journaling patches, ribbons and bows. Snowflakes, baubles and wreaths also make nice circular frames. Just cut out an inner circle leaving a frame.

Small images of snowflakes, baubles and stars make great accents too. Collect your scrap elements in plastic bags according to theme or function. Bits of used wrapping paper make nice backgrounds.

The stocking project has a template, but there are no templates for the page and card projects. I have included the examples of projects made with used Holiday cards to serve as inspiration. You can copy the layouts or design your own.

For selling, make some nice samples to show. Plastic sleeves in a file can be viewed and paged if you're short on table space. Sell the loose frames, elements and word strips in packets. Or prepare base units of cards, postcards, stockings or pages. Then add the loose elements in a packet so the purchaser can finish it at home with personal photos.

PROJECT 41- PHOTO POSTCARD

Very Easy

Example for inspiration. No templates for this project.

PROJECT 42 - PHOTO STOCKINGS

Easy

Template is on Sheet 22

These photo stockings are a fun variation on scrapbook pages.

Adapt the toe and heel sections of the stocking template to make use of circular elements. Use portrait frame cards for the top section of the boot. The stocking can be made taller by adding more elements.

Add scrapbook tags or word strips for flair and messages. Pictures of baubles add a festive note, and wreaths make nice photo tags.

The stockings can be used as scrapbook stocking garlands for the hearth, walls or shelves. Just keep away from open flames!

PROJECT 43 - SCRAPBOOK PAGE

Very Easy

Example for inspiration. No templates for this project.

Make pages in standard 8" x 8" or 12" x 12" pages to fit in regular scrapbook albums.

Bits of wrapping paper are useful to use as backing papers. Frame the page to size, or first add a border of wrapping paper or plain card around the page.

PROJECT 44 - SQUARE PHOTO CARD

Very Easy

Example for inspiration. No templates for this project.

Make a scrapbook photo frame from a greeting card with a frame or border design, and use wreaths and baubles as round photo frames.

TIP: Make envelopes from leftover wrapping paper for the photo cards and postcards.

PROJECT 45 - STAR STACK

Easy

Template is on Sheet 21

The dimensional star stack is great for using up odd images.

Only the edge of each star is visible. A good idea is to have contrast of color or light and dark between the layers. The topmost star needs to have an identifiable image – and it could also be a photograph.

For wall or tree decorations, place foam squares between the layers to raise each layer. It can also be placed in a scrapbook. Don't raise the layers for scrapbooks, however, as the element will become too thick.

Add a looped ribbon and bow to make a nice tree decoration. Two stacked stars can also be glued back-to-back to make a fully round 3D ornament that can be viewed from the front or back.

PROJECT 46 - ADVENT POSTER

Takes Time

Advent Numbers are on Sheet 38

1	7	13	19
2	8	14	20
3	9	15	21
4	10	16	22
5	11	17	23
6	12	18	24

This is an ideal school project, because you need 24 door and/ or window cards. The doors or windows open to reveal a number.

Purchased cardstock is needed for the backing of the poster. The printable numbers can correspond to candy, or coins. A story per day is also a good suggestion for children. Each number then corresponds to a story or book. This project will also look great in an unglazed frame. The numbers are in the template section.

INSTRUCTIONS

- Start with your tallest window/door card and measure the length.
- Then choose the card with the widest image.
- Combine the two measurements to get a rectangle for the master measurement.
- Take a poster-sized piece of cardstock and divide it into 24 rectangles according to the master measurement. You might have to add to the poster sheet.
- You can divide the sheet into two by twelve sections for a tall poster, or three by eight, four by six etc. You can even make a long continuous Advent border.
- Cut three sides of each door or window image so it can open.
- Glue a door or window card in each rectangle. Don't glue the sections that open.
- It doesn't matter if some smaller cards have lots of white space around them. Decorate white areas with elements if you wish. Wrapping paper off-cuts can be used as backing for smaller cards too.
- Paste a number from 1 to 24 to the poster on the inside of each open door or window. Windows can open from the center if the card depicts window or door pairs.

PROJECT 47- NOEL WALL TEXT

Easy

Template is on Sheets 27, 28, 29 and 30

Lavish cards depicting paintings by the Old Masters are perfect for this project.

Included are templates for an easy to cut font, but you can print out the letters from any computer font that is easy to cut out.

There are letter templates for the word NOEL, but if you print them out yourself, the text can be changed to holiday messages such as: PEACE, HAPPY XMAS, HO-HO-HO etc. The images can be adapted to fit the message and you can choose your language.

The letters N, E and L each fit on a 5" x 7" card, but the O template needs two 7" x 5" cards. It is assembled from two portrait images or two landscape images that are glued together via little tabs. Or you can place the O on an open card and make use of the back of the card for half of the O. The blank section can then be decorated.

PROJECT 48 - ANGEL COLLAGE

Easy

Template is on Sheet 24

Gather nice word strips, angel and star images and purchased cardstock in any size.

You can really get creative with this one! The poster only serves as an example.

The cards with lavish paintings of angels are perfect, but as with all these projects, any images will do. The shapes of the angels are well defined to form a nice silhouette regardless of imagery.

Those typical images of musical instruments and greenery are great for this, but the angel template also has its own optional trumpet. Small angel silhouettes are also included on Sheet 16. Use the angel as a card topper too.

Feel free to include doves from the Dove project; hearts form the Heart Sachet and stars from the Cookie Plate or Star Stack. You can even use trees from the tree projects to form a ground line. Add word strips and Christmas messages cut from cards with prominent text.

PROJECT 49 - PEACE DOVES WALL ART

Easy

Template is on Sheet 24

Many Holiday cards depict Peace Doves and they are perfect for this project.

The dove silhouette has a clear shape, so the images can also be cut from any Holiday picture cards. A variety of dove sizes are included in the template collection. The doves can be combined with stars, angels, and hearts from the other templates. The small images on Sheet 16 also make nice tags and gift toppers.

The dove cut-outs can simply be arranged on the wall and stuck on with wall putty. Or use them to make framed art and posters.

They can also be used as tree decorations, or strung along in a garland by punching a hole in the head and tail sections or a single hole through the top of the wing.

A single dove can be glued to the back of a used card to make a new postcard.

And the images can be glued around the rim of a paper plate to make a wreath.
Cut out the center of a paper plate and follow the instructions for the Cookie Plate.

PROJECT 50 - HOLIDAY BUNTING

Very Easy

Template is on Sheet 8

This is an easy and gorgeous project for little flags that can be used year after year.

A medley of mismatched cards is used to great effect. You will need a lot of cards to make a good length of bunting, so the project is ideal for group and class projects and is a super way of repurposing loads of donated cards!

The flags are joined by weaving a long length of ribbon through punched holes, but fasteners as were used for the Zigzag border can be used for this project too. Edges can also be cut with decorative scissors and the edges can be finished with glitter.

White flags from the back of cards or discarded envelopes can have picture cut-outs and words glued to them for a charming and stylish alternative.
Bunting is enjoying a big revival and this is sure to be a popular item to sell.

Also use the free printable gingham pages to great effect by cutting bunting from them to combine with pictures and text from cards.

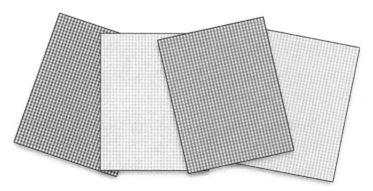

I hope you enjoy making these crafts to recycle and repurpose used Christmas cards.

Please send me photos of your makes - I want to start an inspiration gallery on Anni Arts!

BONUS PROJECTS AND FREEBIES

Get your *bonus projects, printable set of templates* and pages *of Anni Arts printable pattern paper* featuring gingham designs in Lime, Red, Xmas Green and Ochre.
Also get *the second blank template collection* to decorate with bits and pics from used Christmas and Holiday cards. The blank set has no surface lines or text on them.

-Access them with your email address and receipt number at *Anni Arts*
http://www.anniarts.com.

Bonus Templates for: Door Sign, CD Sleeve, Bottle Tie, Sticky Notes Topper, Poinsettia Parcel Decoration and Reusable Place Cards - Plus a larger Tissue Pack and Choc Wrap

-Get more free blank Craft Templates that you can use for recycling Christmas card projects by 'Liking' the *Anni Arts Facebook Page*. "Like" Templates include frames, toppers, card, envelope, tag and bag. Use with the free printable paper.

-And *Anni Arts Crafts* - my printable crafts site - has stacks more freebies to download!
If you have any problems obtaining the templates, contact me at anniarts.com

ABOUT THE AUTHOR

Anni Lipsanen is a professional graphic designer and illustrator with more than twenty five years of experience in the fields of illustration, packaging, book design, corporate identity, paper crafts and product design. Her graphic design and publication site is Anni Arts (at www.anniarts.com).

In recent years she also started to design and illustrate paper crafts and downloadable printables for card making, gift packs and scrapbooking that are available from her Anni Arts Crafts web site (at www.anniartscrafts.com).

She is also an enthusiastic recycler and loves to create projects to repurpose and upcycle used items. Hence this book to recycle used Christmas cards.

Her motto - in business and in life - is:

CREATE SOMETHING BEAUTIFUL

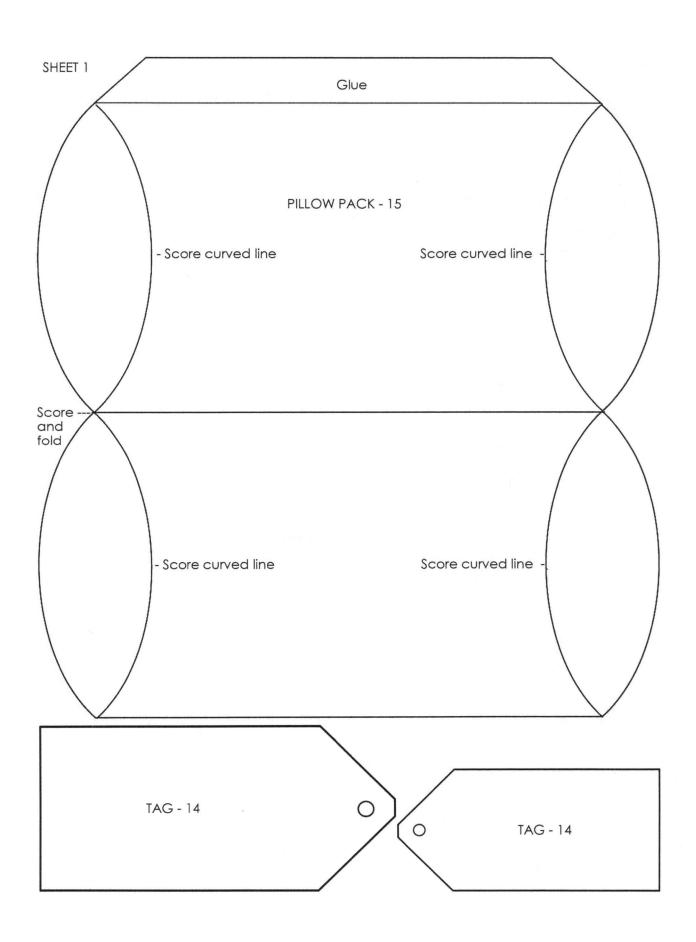

SHEET 1

Glue

PILLOW PACK - 15

- Score curved line

Score curved line -

Score ---
and
fold

- Score curved line

Score curved line -

TAG - 14

TAG - 14

SHEET 2

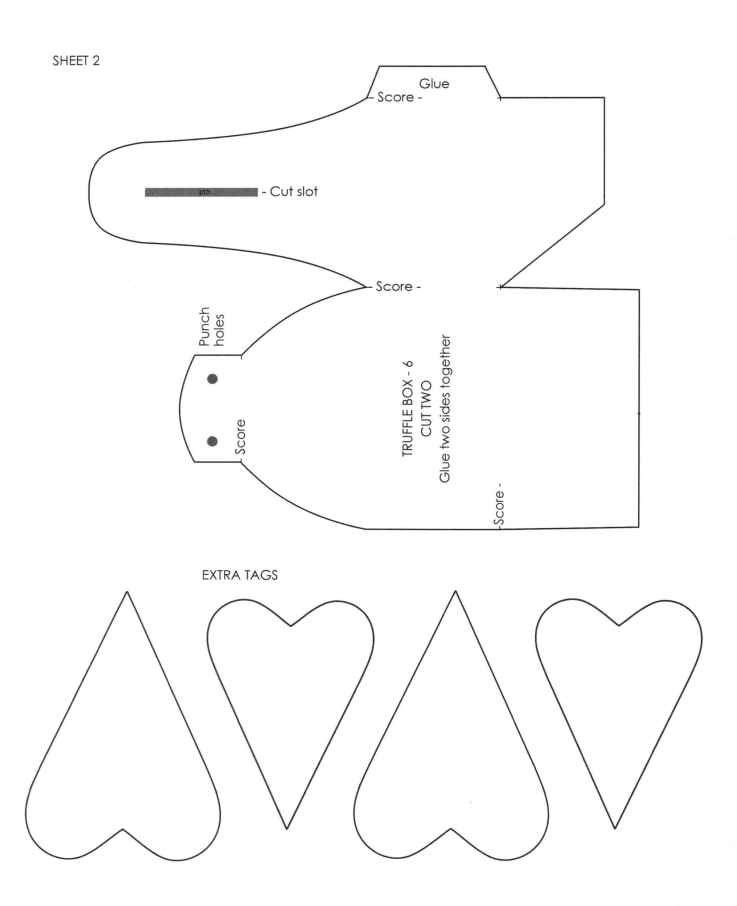

Glue

— Score -

Cut — - Cut slot

Punch holes

Score

TRUFFLE BOX - 6
CUT TWO
Glue two sides together

— Score -

— Score -

EXTRA TAGS

SHEET 3

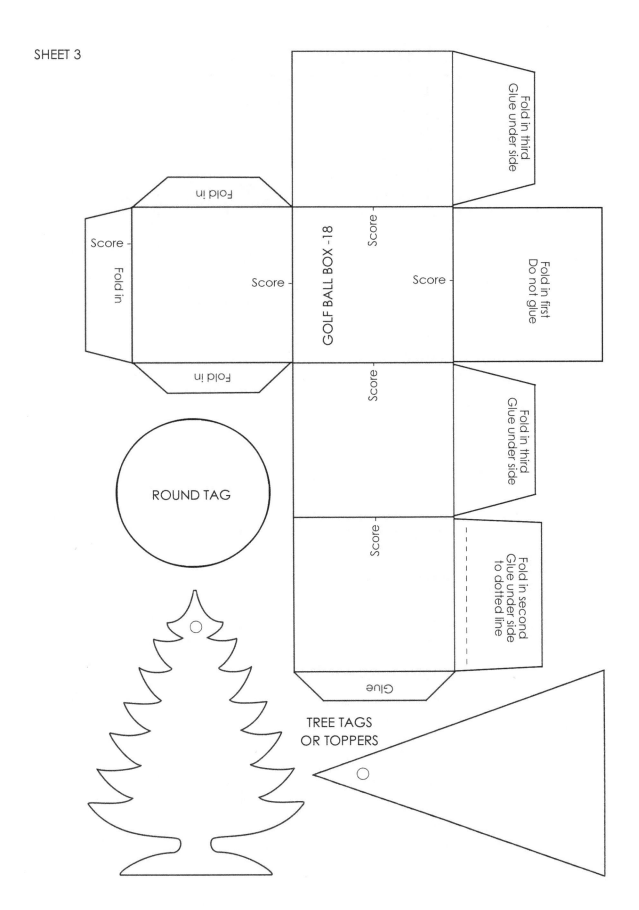

Fold in third
Glue under side

GOLF BALL BOX -18

Score

Score

Score

Score

Fold in

Score

Fold in

Fold in

Fold in first
Do not glue

Fold in third
Glue under side

ROUND TAG

Score

Fold in second
Glue under side
to dotted line

Glue

TREE TAGS
OR TOPPERS

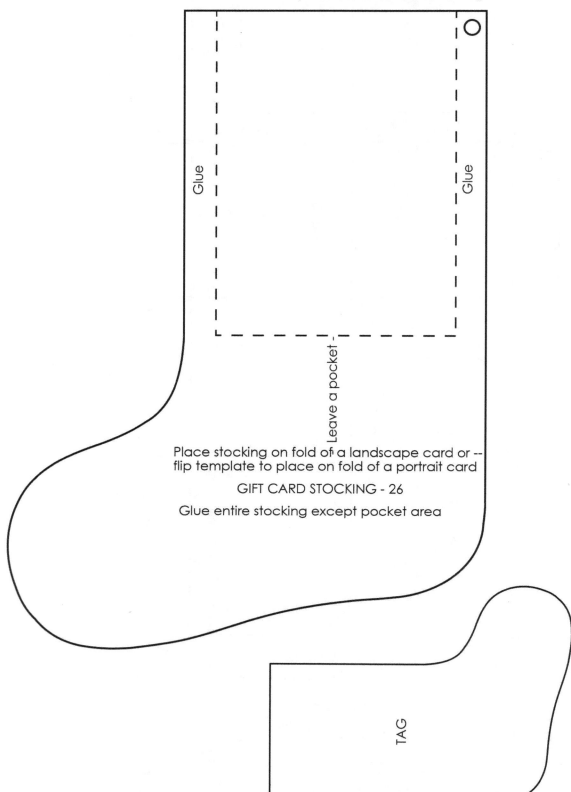

Optional hole for ribbon or tag

Glue

Glue

Leave a pocket

Place stocking on fold of a landscape card or --
flip template to place on fold of a portrait card

GIFT CARD STOCKING - 26

Glue entire stocking except pocket area

TAG

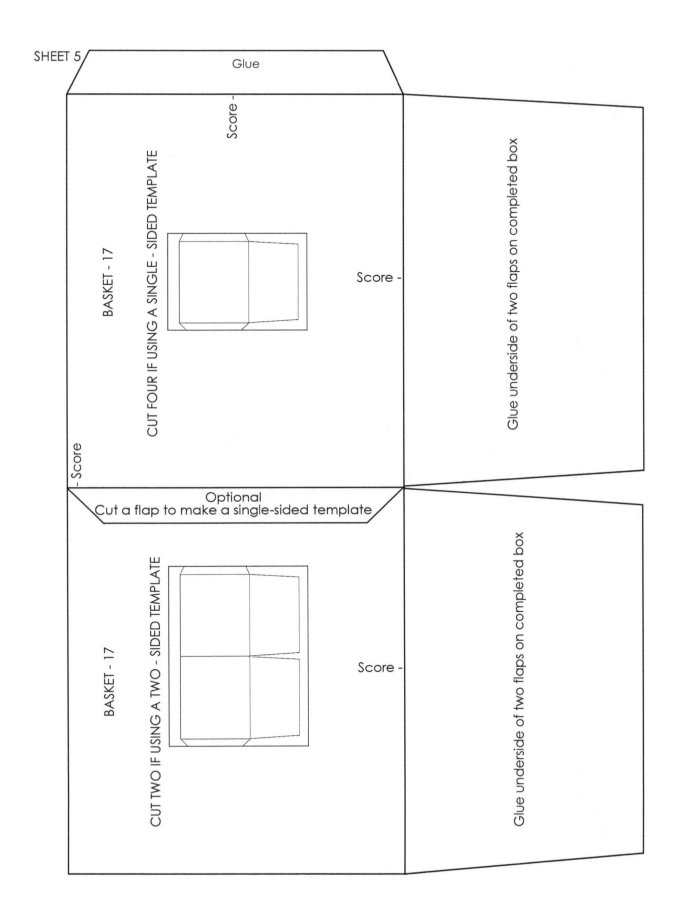

SHEET 5

Glue

Score -

BASKET - 17

CUT FOUR IF USING A SINGLE - SIDED TEMPLATE

Score -

Glue underside of two flaps on completed box

- Score

Optional
Cut a flap to make a single-sided template

BASKET - 17

CUT TWO IF USING A TWO - SIDED TEMPLATE

Score -

Glue underside of two flaps on completed box

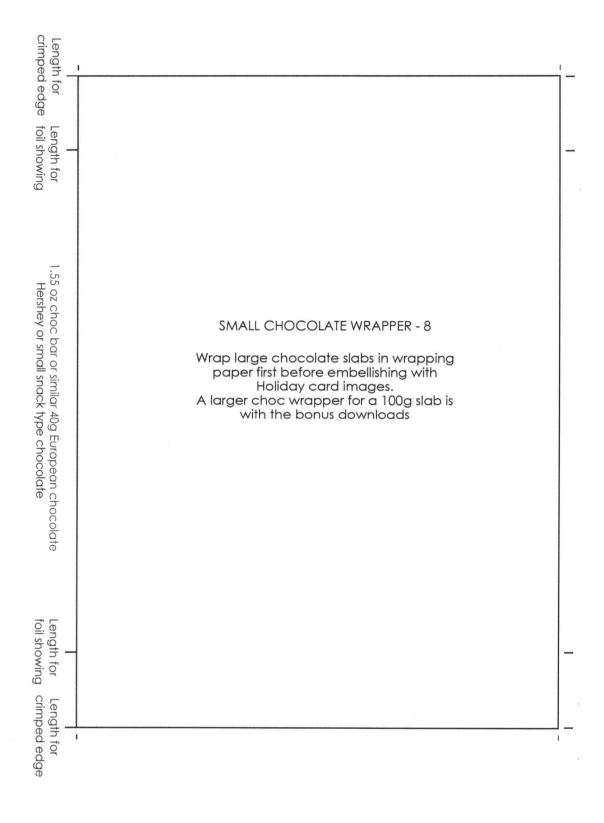

Length for crimped edge
Length for foil showing

1.55 oz choc bar or similar 40g European chocolate
Hershey or small snack type chocolate

SMALL CHOCOLATE WRAPPER - 8

Wrap large chocolate slabs in wrapping paper first before embellishing with Holiday card images.
A larger choc wrapper for a 100g slab is with the bonus downloads

Length for foil showing
Length for crimped edge

SHEET 7

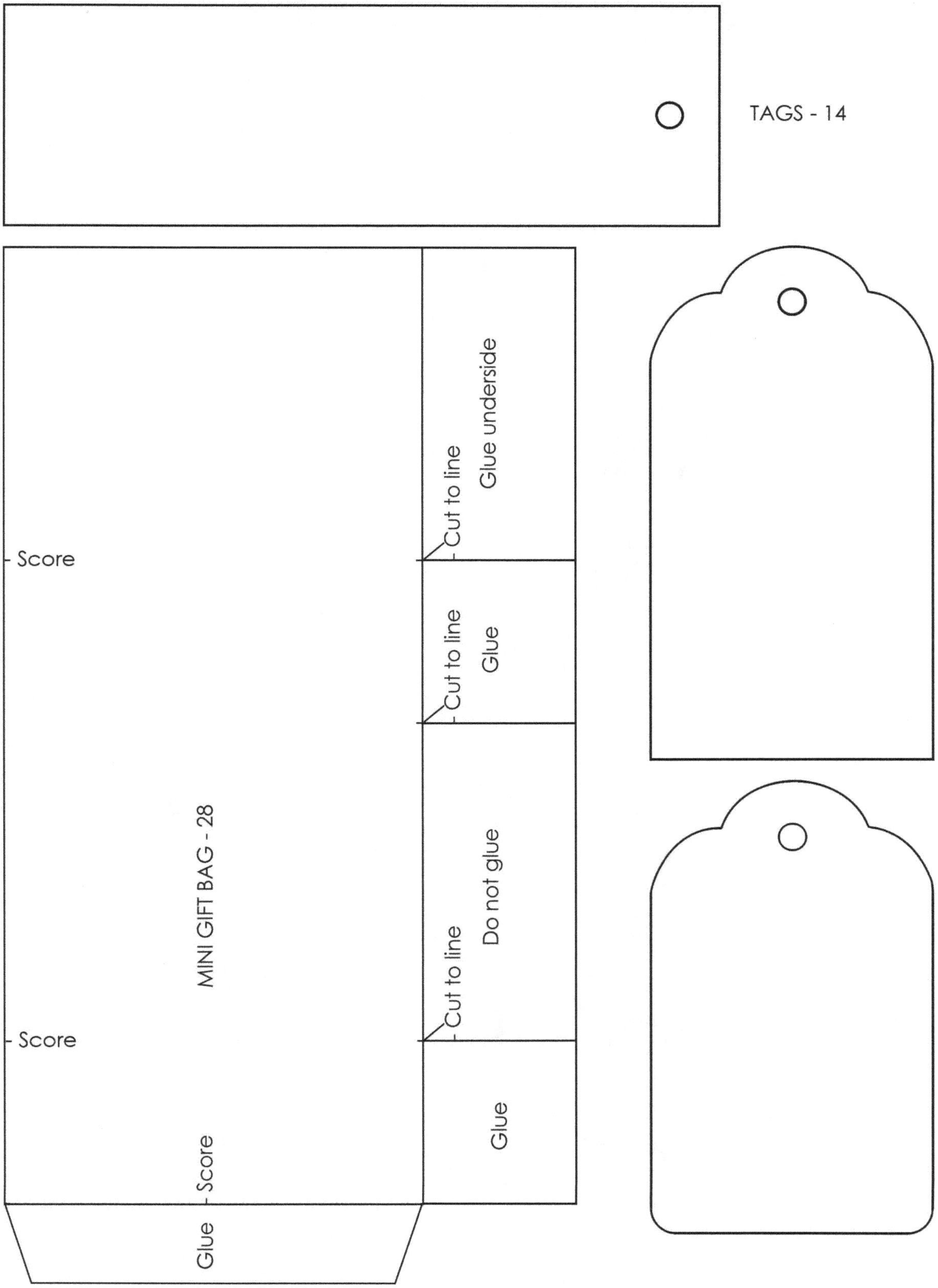

TAGS - 14

Score

Score

Score

Glue

MINI GIFT BAG - 28

Glue

Cut to line

Glue underside

Cut to line

Glue

Cut to line

Do not glue

Cut to line

Glue

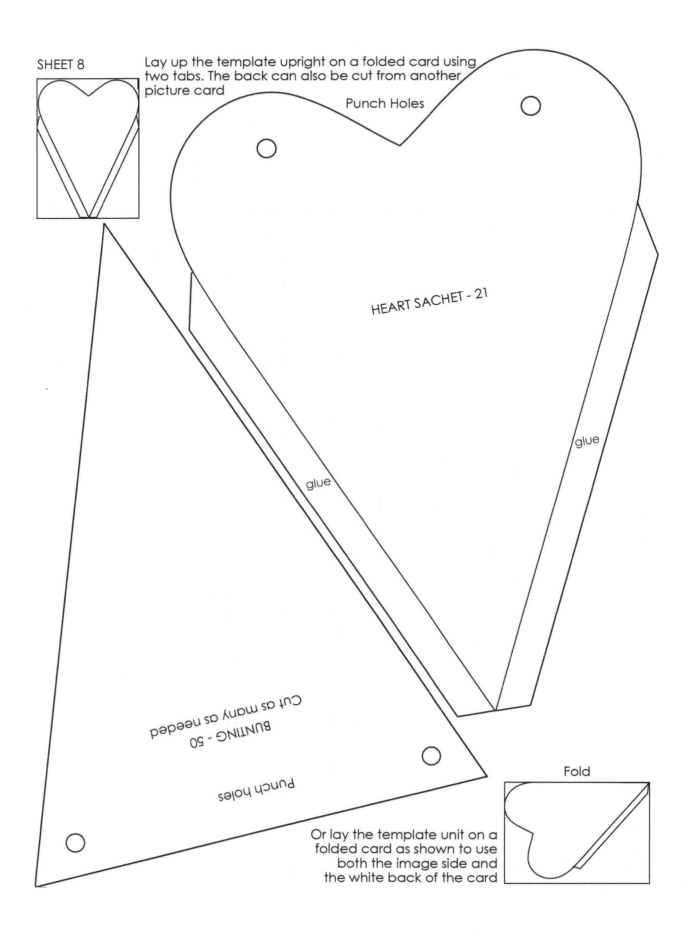

SHEET 8

Lay up the template upright on a folded card using two tabs. The back can also be cut from another picture card

Punch Holes

HEART SACHET - 21

glue

glue

Cut as many as needed
BUNTING - 50

Punch holes

Fold

Or lay the template unit on a folded card as shown to use both the image side and the white back of the card

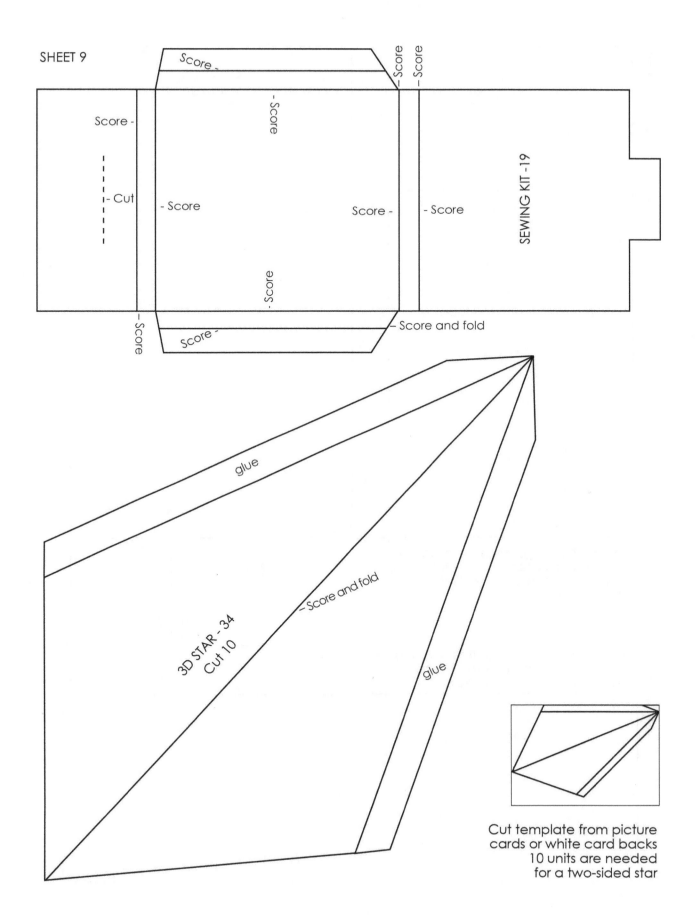

SHEET 9

SEWING KIT - 19

Score -
- Cut
- Score
Score -
- Score
- Score
Score -
Score -
Score
- Score
Score
- Score
- Score
Score -
- Score and fold
Score -

3D STAR - 34
Cut 10

glue
- Score and fold
glue

Cut template from picture
cards or white card backs
10 units are needed
for a two-sided star

Ribbon slit
cut out

Ribbon slit
cut out

Cut out for
address label

LUGGAGE TAG - 14

The luggage tag needs an image on
both sides, so choose an overall design
or a picture that can be divided into a
front and back

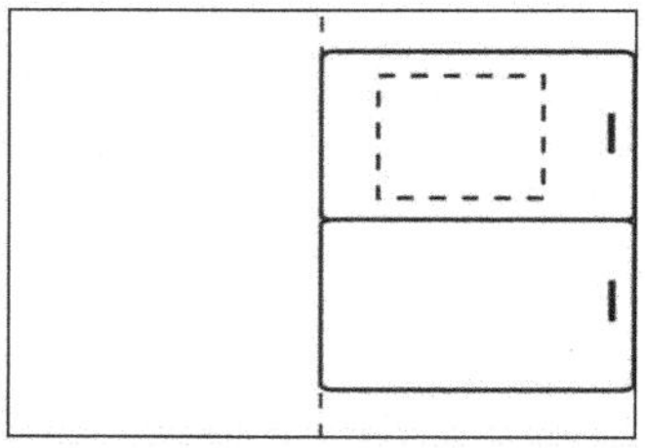

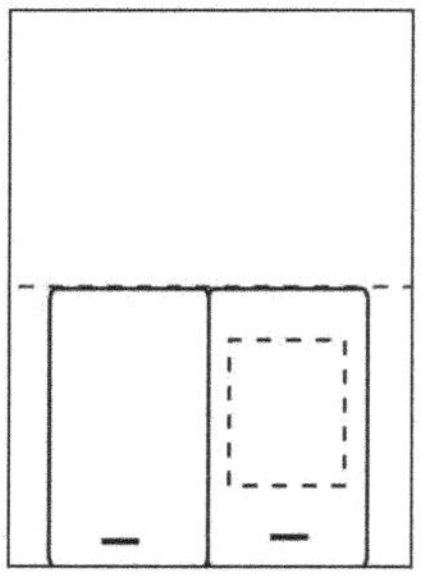

The size for the serviette ring is optional,
so adapt the template to be longer,
shorter or narrower as needed

SERVIETTE RING - 10

Glue

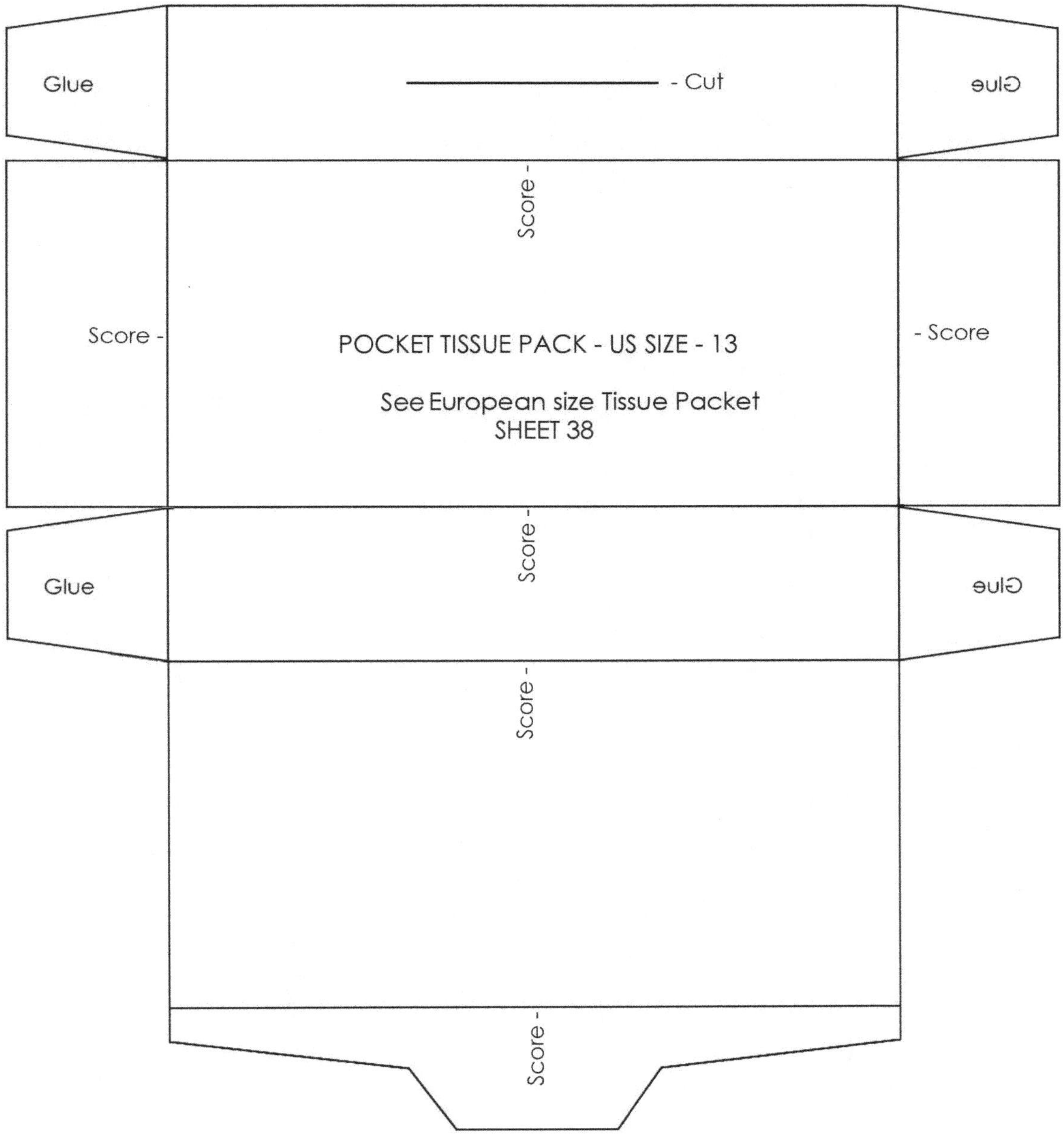

Glue

————————————— - Cut

Score -

Score - POCKET TISSUE PACK - US SIZE - 13

See European size Tissue Packet
SHEET 38

- Score

Glue

Glue

Score -

Score -

Score -

BOOKMARK -14

○

Each bauble needs four strips.
The cardstock that postcards are printed on, is generally too thick for this project,
so keep greeting cards that are printed on lighter card or paper for the baubles.

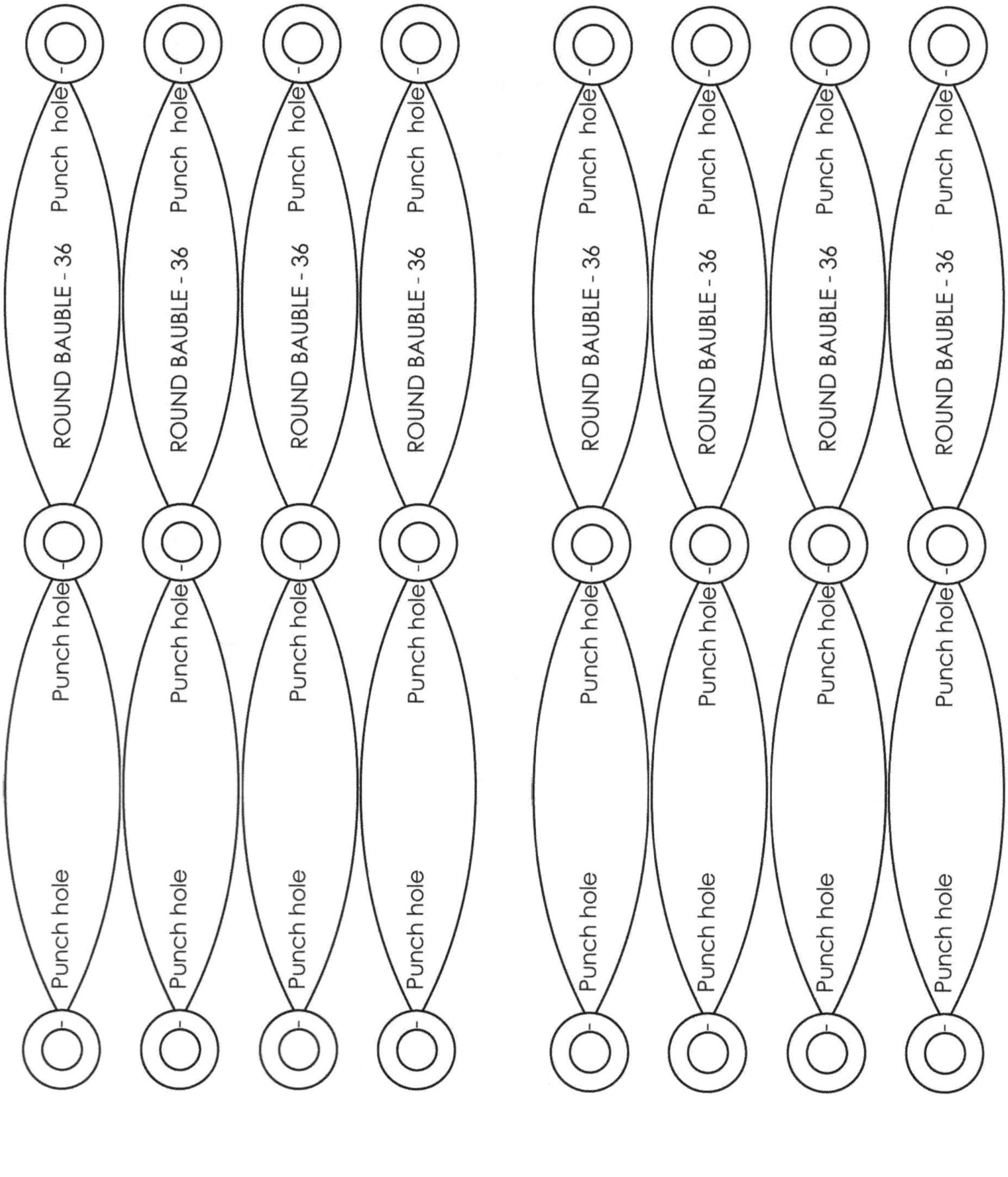

ROUND BAUBLE - 36   Punch hole

Punch hole

Punch hole

- Score and wrap to back of candle pair

CANDLE SLEEVE - 23

- Score and wrap to back of candle pair

The sleeve must be cut from a card that is 5 inches across to wrap around two candles.
The length can be 7 inches long - or adapt the length as needed.

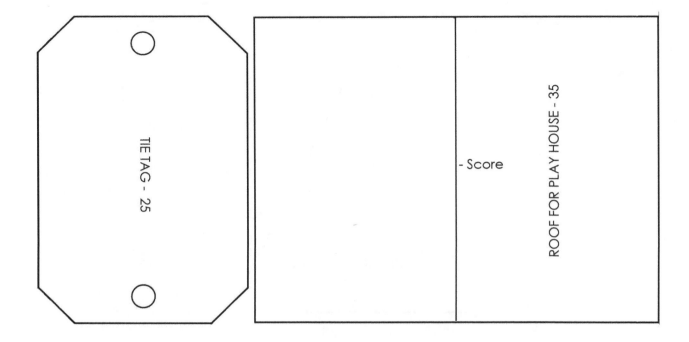

TIE TAG - 25

- Score

ROOF FOR PLAY HOUSE - 35

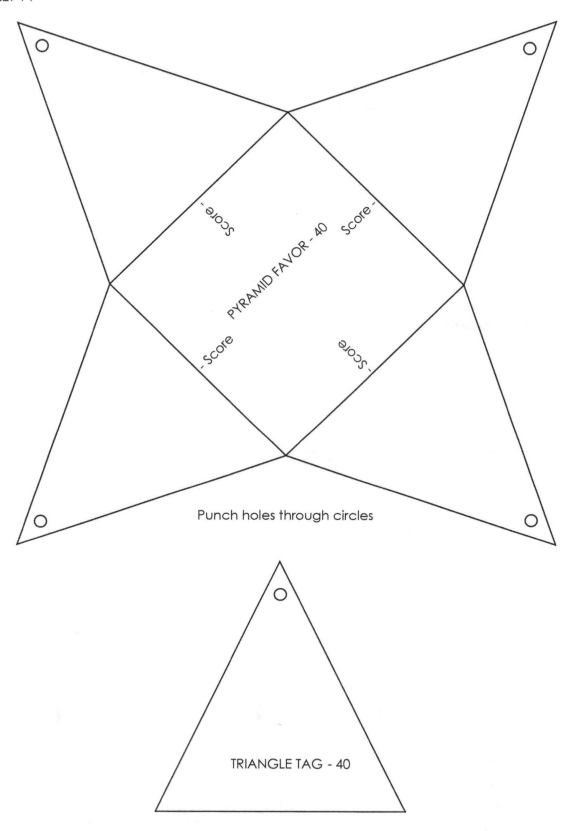

PYRAMID FAVOR - 40

Score -

Score -

- Score

- Score

Punch holes through circles

TRIANGLE TAG - 40

SHEET 15

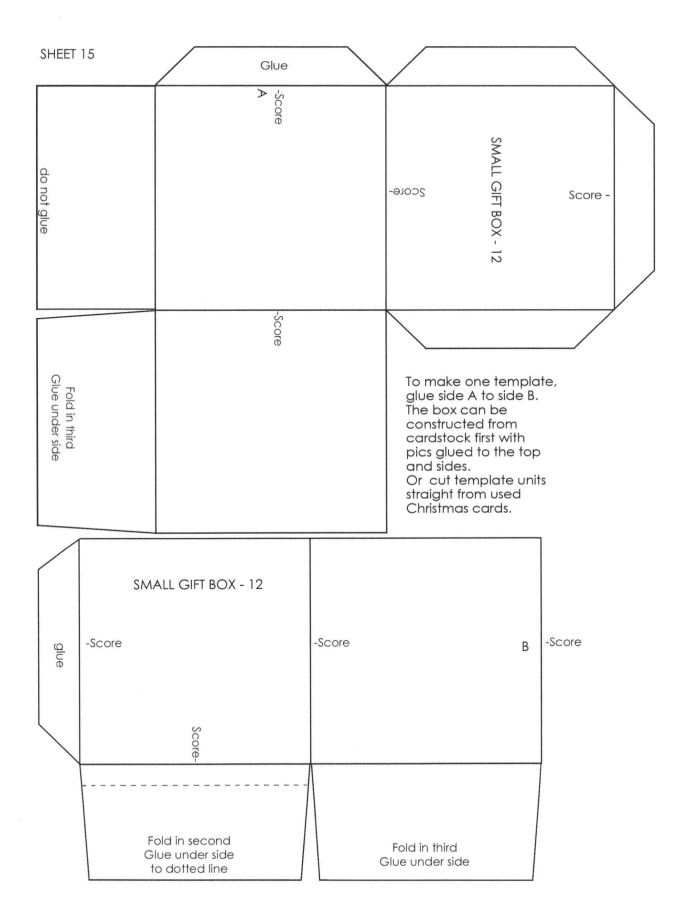

Glue

A

-Score

-Score

Score-

SMALL GIFT BOX - 12

Score -

do not glue

-Score

Fold in third
Glue under side

To make one template,
glue side A to side B.
The box can be
constructed from
cardstock first with
pics glued to the top
and sides.
Or cut template units
straight from used
Christmas cards.

SMALL GIFT BOX - 12

glue

-Score

-Score

B

-Score

Score-

Fold in second
Glue under side
to dotted line

Fold in third
Glue under side

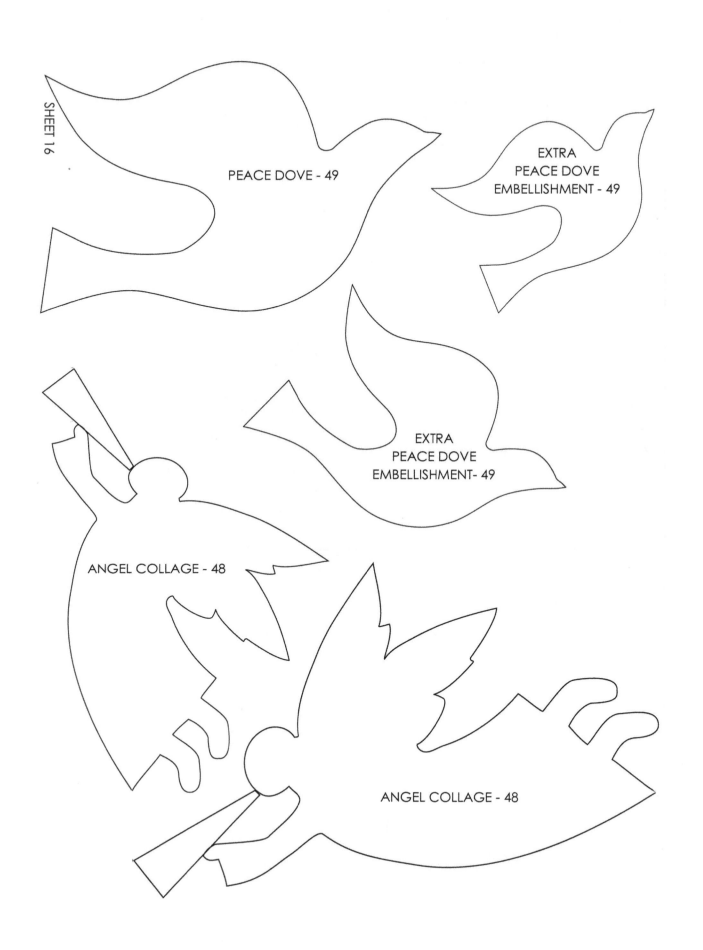

SHEET 16

PEACE DOVE - 49

EXTRA
PEACE DOVE
EMBELLISHMENT - 49

EXTRA
PEACE DOVE
EMBELLISHMENT- 49

ANGEL COLLAGE - 48

ANGEL COLLAGE - 48

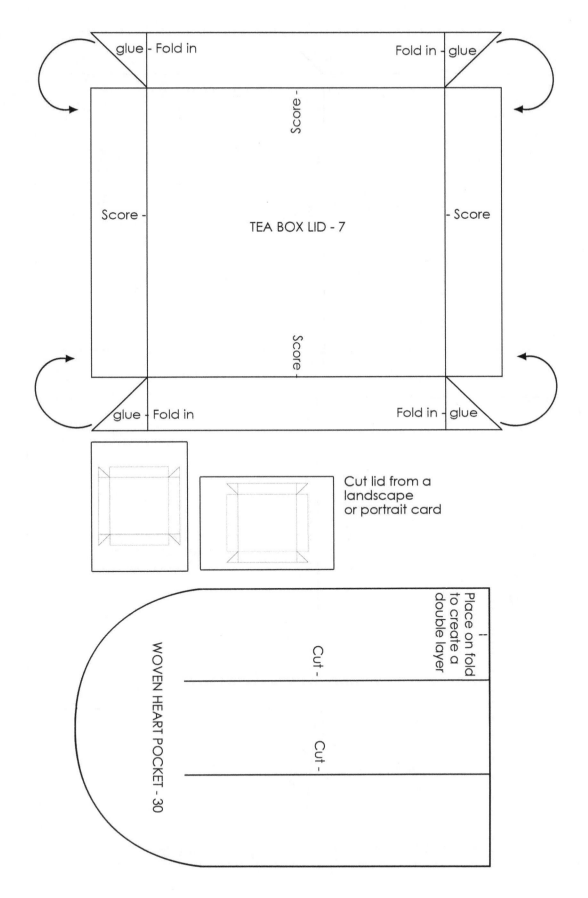

glue - Fold in   Fold in - glue

Score -

Score -   - Score

TEA BOX LID - 7

Score -

glue - Fold in   Fold in - glue

Cut lid from a
landscape
or portrait card

Place on fold
to create a
double layer

Cut -

Cut -

WOVEN HEART POCKET - 30

SHEET 18

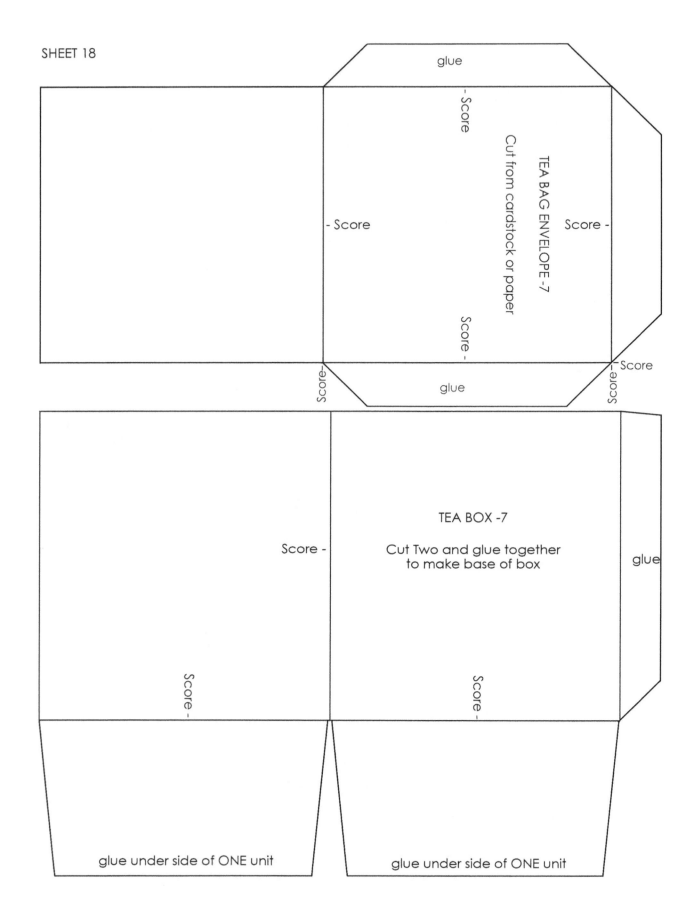

glue

- Score

- Score

TEA BAG ENVELOPE -7

Cut from cardstock or paper

Score -

Score -

Score -

Score

glue

Score -

TEA BOX -7

Cut Two and glue together
to make base of box

glue

Score -

Score -

Score -

glue under side of ONE unit

glue under side of ONE unit

SHEET 19

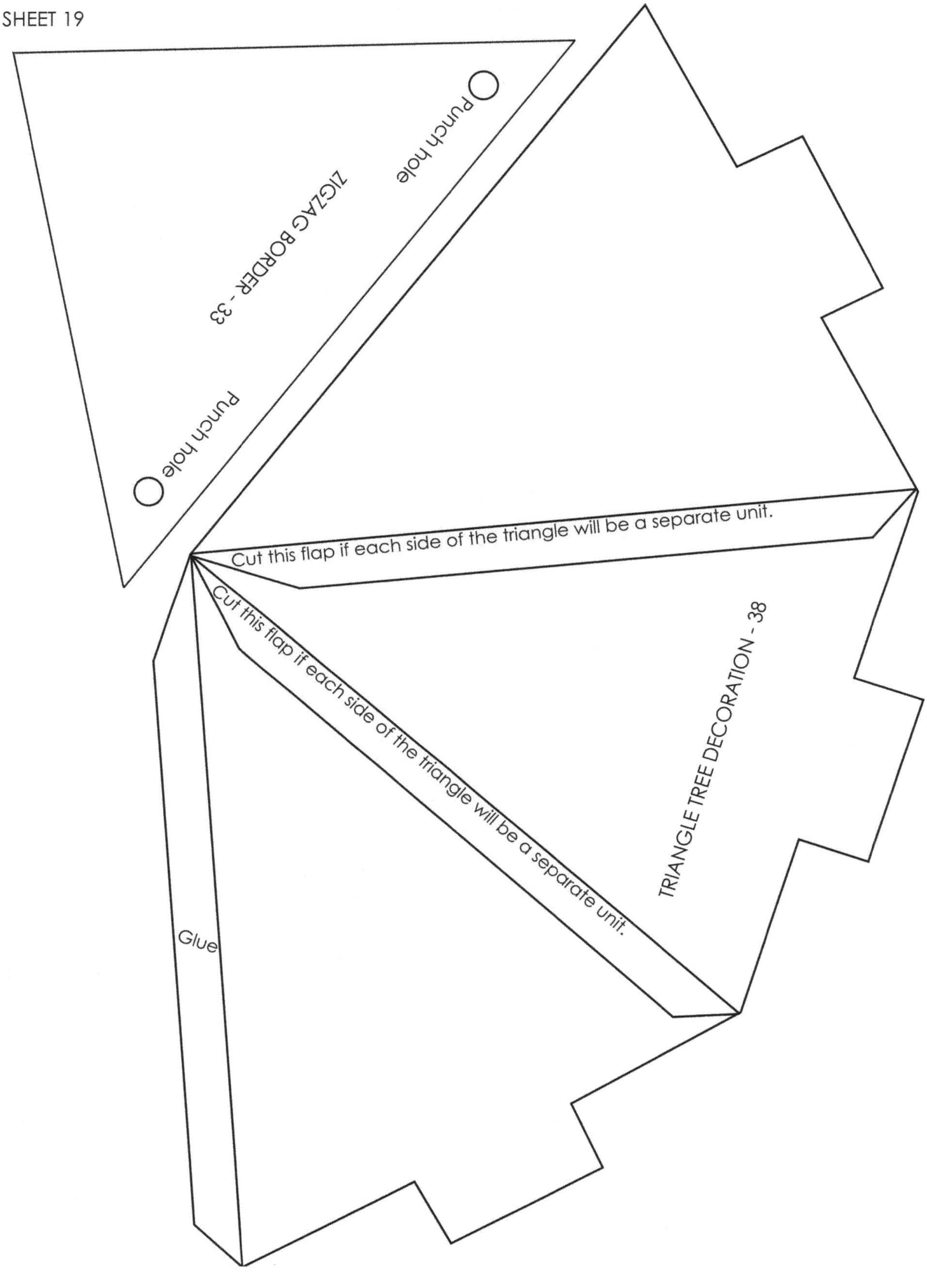

ZIGZAG BORDER - 33
Punch hole
Punch hole
TRIANGLE TREE DECORATION - 38
Cut this flap if each side of the triangle will be a separate unit.
Cut this flap if each side of the triangle will be a separate unit.
Glue

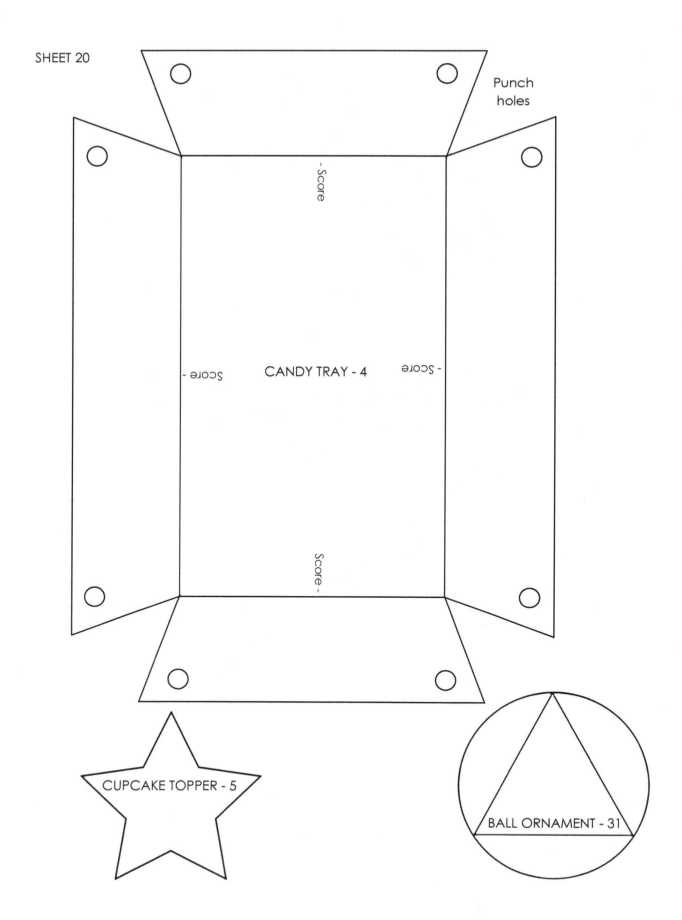

SHEET 20

Punch holes

- Score

- Score -

- Score -

CANDY TRAY - 4

Score -

CUPCAKE TOPPER - 5

BALL ORNAMENT - 31

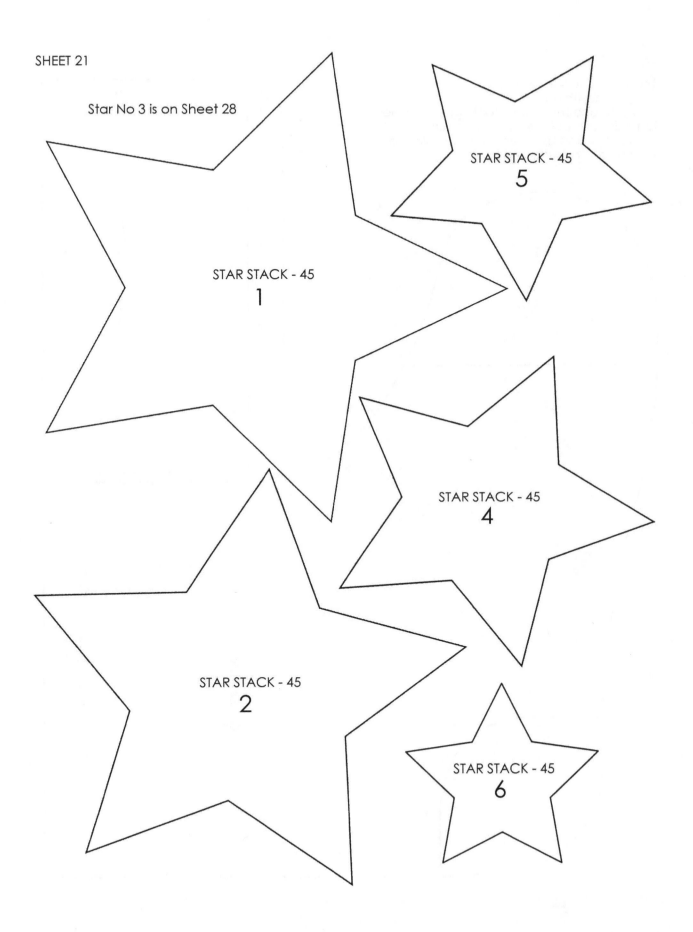

SHEET 21

Star No 3 is on Sheet 28

STAR STACK - 45
1

STAR STACK - 45
5

STAR STACK - 45
4

STAR STACK - 45
2

STAR STACK - 45
6

SHEET 22

The template is in two parts.
Lengthen with unit B.
You can also make the stocking even taller -
just add as much as you want to unit A.
Adapt toe and heel section according to
your scrapbook elements.

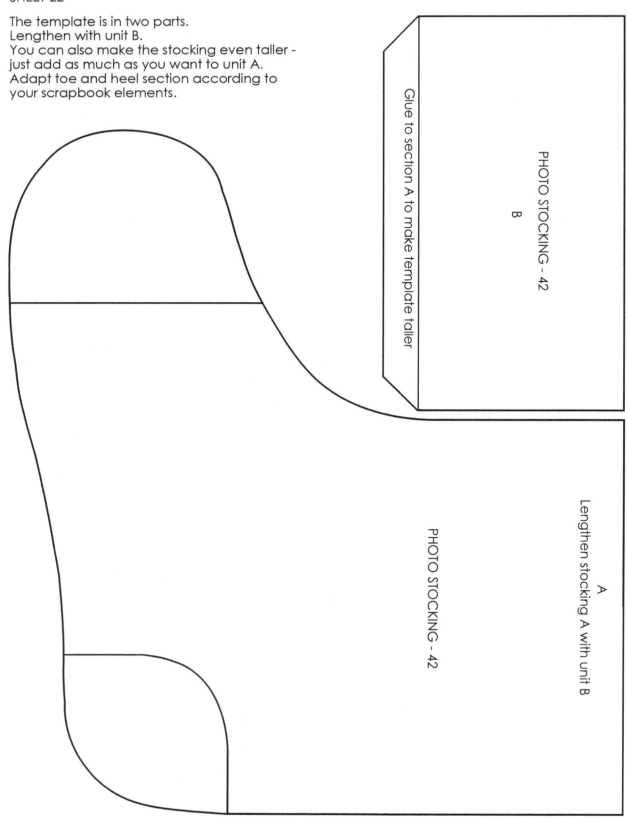

Glue to section A to make template taller

PHOTO STOCKING - 42

B

Lengthen stocking A with unit B

A

PHOTO STOCKING - 42

The four box template units can be glued
together to make a large template to cut
from cardstock or can be used in units of
four to cut from four different greeting cards

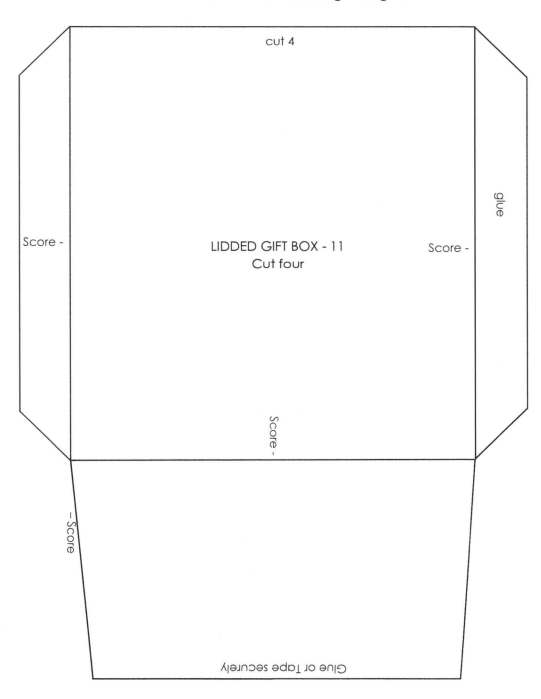

cut 4

glue

Score -   Score -

LIDDED GIFT BOX - 11
Cut four

Score -

– Score

Glue or tape securely

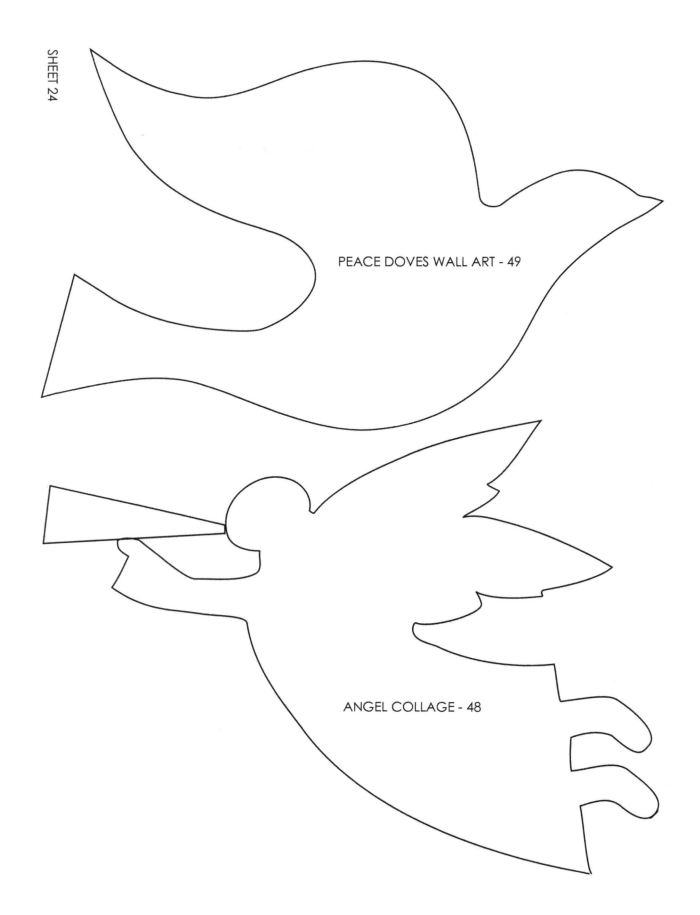

PEACE DOVES WALL ART - 49

ANGEL COLLAGE - 48

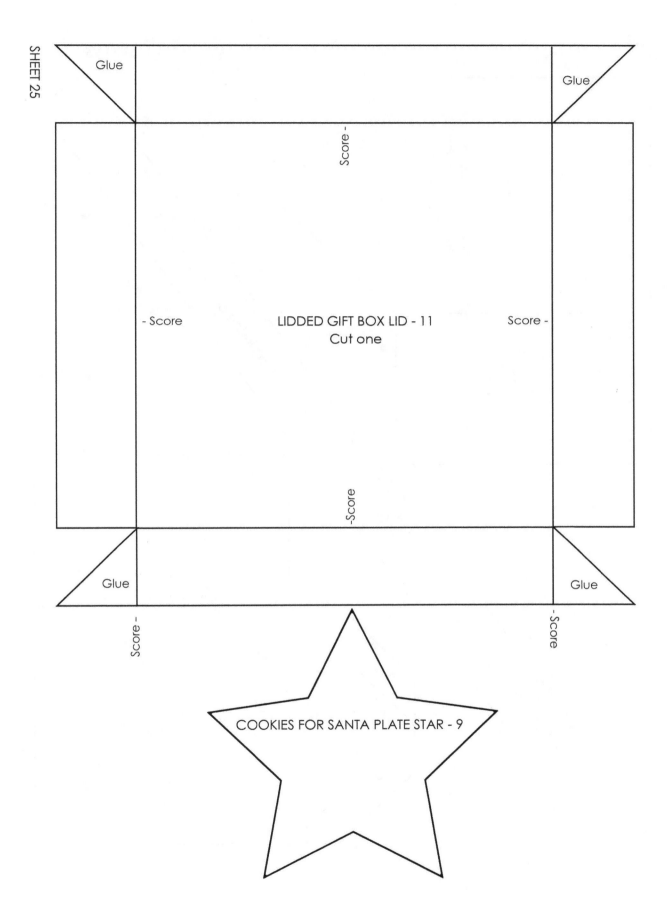

Glue

Glue

Score -

- Score

LIDDED GIFT BOX LID - 11
Cut one

Score -

-Score

Glue

Glue

Score -

- Score

COOKIES FOR SANTA PLATE STAR - 9

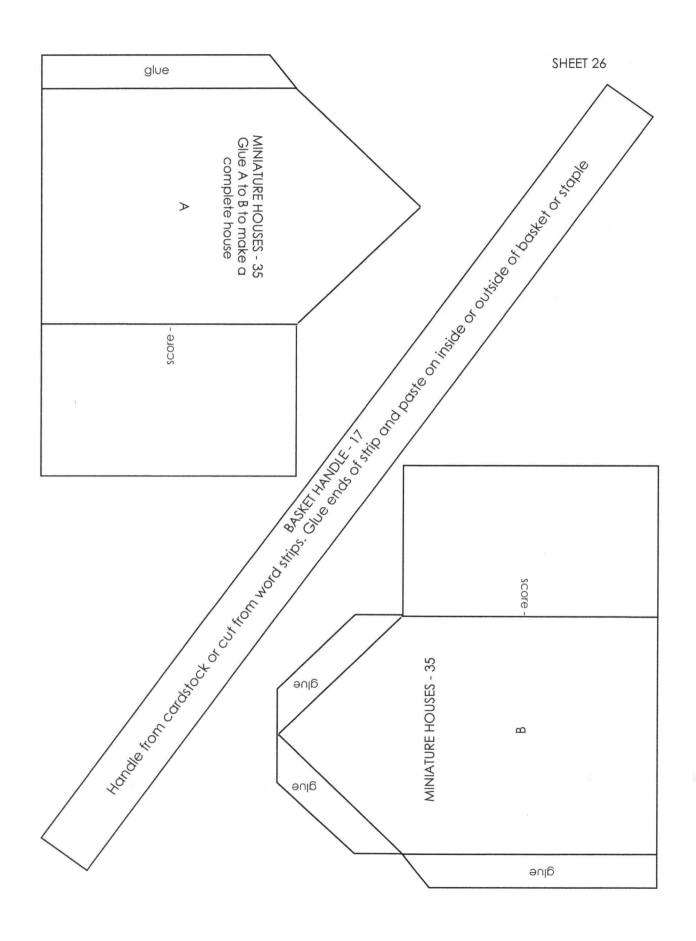

glue

MINIATURE HOUSES - 35
Glue A to B to make a
complete house

A

score -

BASKET HANDLE - 17
Glue ends of strip and paste on inside or outside of basket or staple

Handle from cardstock or cut from word strips.

score -

glue

glue

MINIATURE HOUSES - 35

B

glue

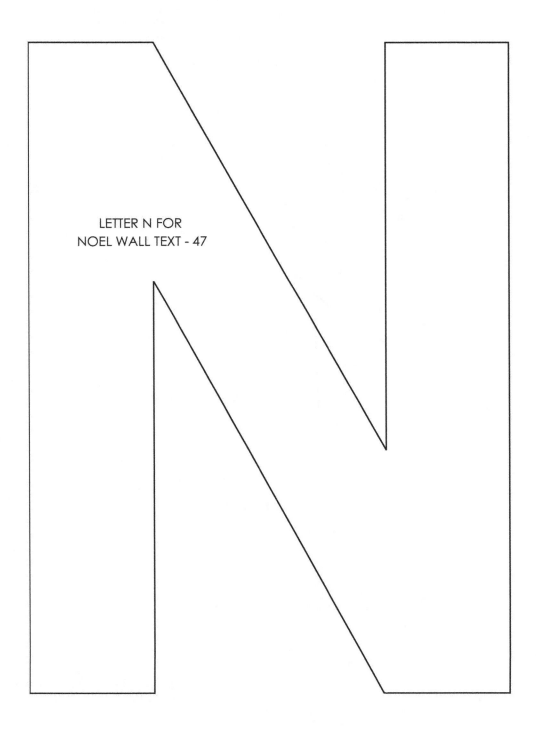

LETTER N FOR
NOEL WALL TEXT - 47

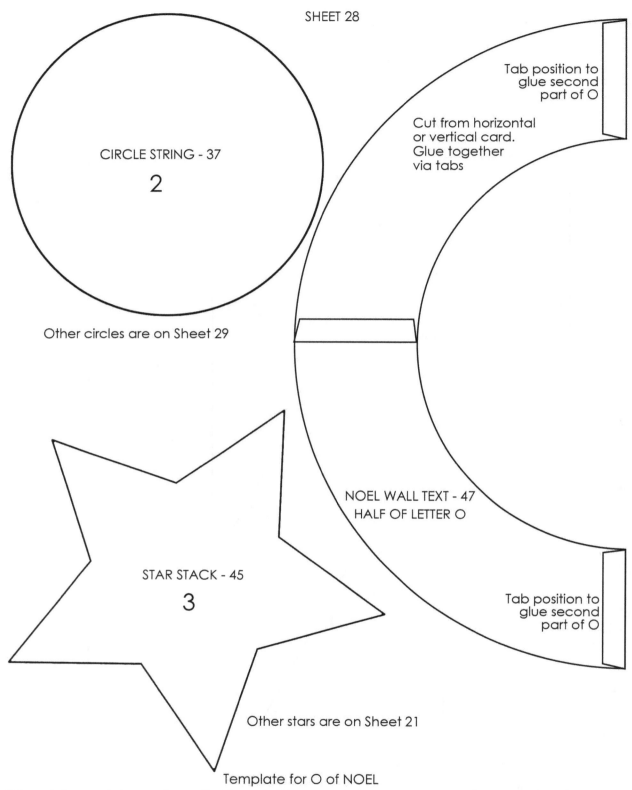

CIRCLE STRING - 37

2

Other circles are on Sheet 29

Tab position to glue second part of O

Cut from horizontal or vertical card. Glue together via tabs

NOEL WALL TEXT - 47
HALF OF LETTER O

Tab position to glue second part of O

STAR STACK - 45

3

Other stars are on Sheet 21

Template for O of NOEL
O template needs two or three 7" x 5" cards. It is assembled from two portrait images or two landscape images that are glued together via the flaps. Or you can simply place the O on an open card and make use of the back of the card too. Decorate the white section. You can also cut another image for the center circle.

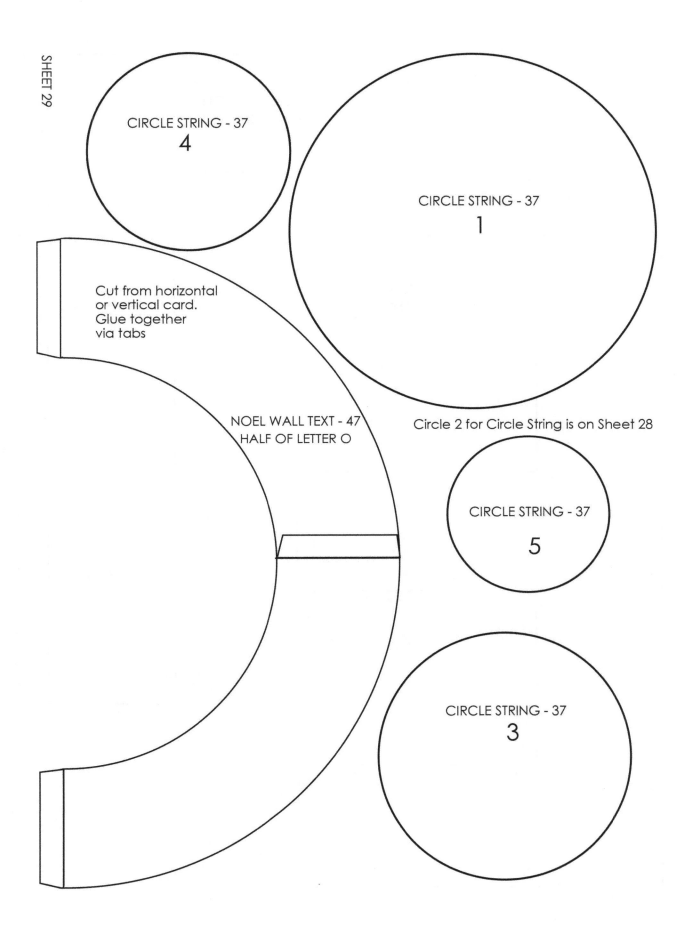

CIRCLE STRING - 37
4

CIRCLE STRING - 37
1

Cut from horizontal
or vertical card.
Glue together
via tabs

NOEL WALL TEXT - 47
HALF OF LETTER O

Circle 2 for Circle String is on Sheet 28

CIRCLE STRING - 37
5

CIRCLE STRING - 37
3

LETTER E FOR
NOEL WALL TEXT - 47

LETTER E FOR
NOEL WALL TEXT - 47

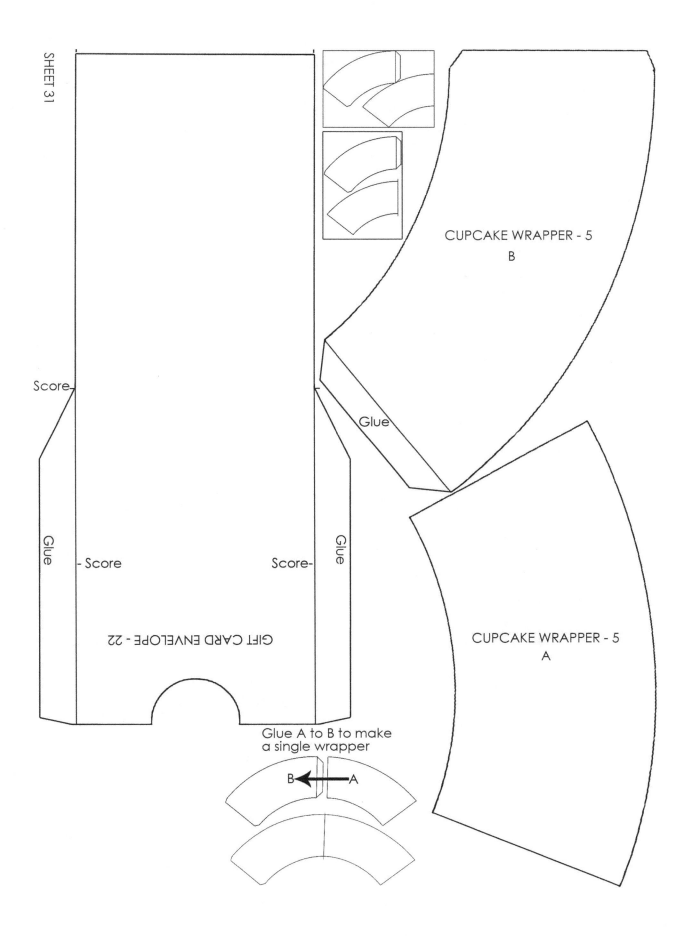

SHEET 31

Score

Glue

Score

Score

Glue

Glue

CUPCAKE WRAPPER - 5
B

Glue

CUPCAKE WRAPPER - 5
A

GIFT CARD ENVELOPE - 22

Glue A to B to make
a single wrapper

B ← A

SHEET 32

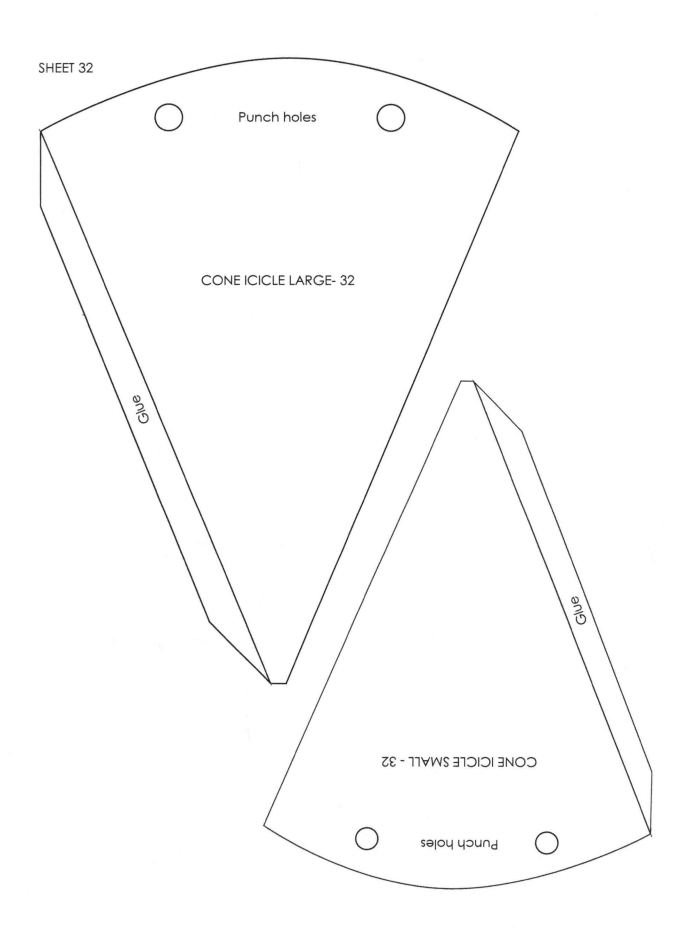

Punch holes

CONE ICICLE LARGE- 32

Glue

Glue

CONE ICICLE SMALL - 32

Punch holes

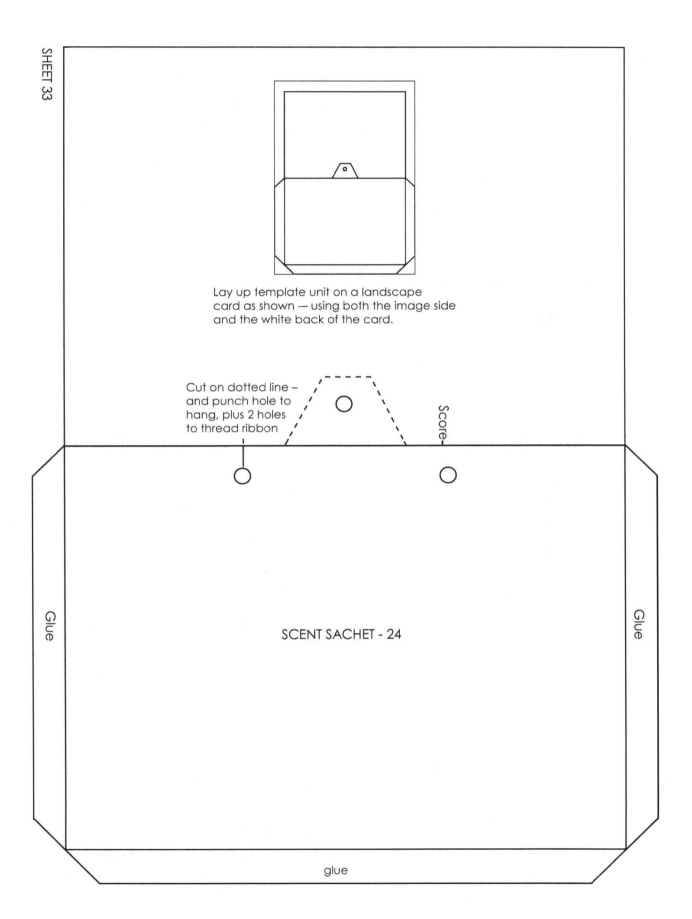

Lay up template unit on a landscape
card as shown — using both the image side
and the white back of the card.

Cut on dotted line –
and punch hole to
hang, plus 2 holes
to thread ribbon

Score

Glue

Glue

SCENT SACHET - 24

glue

SHEET 34

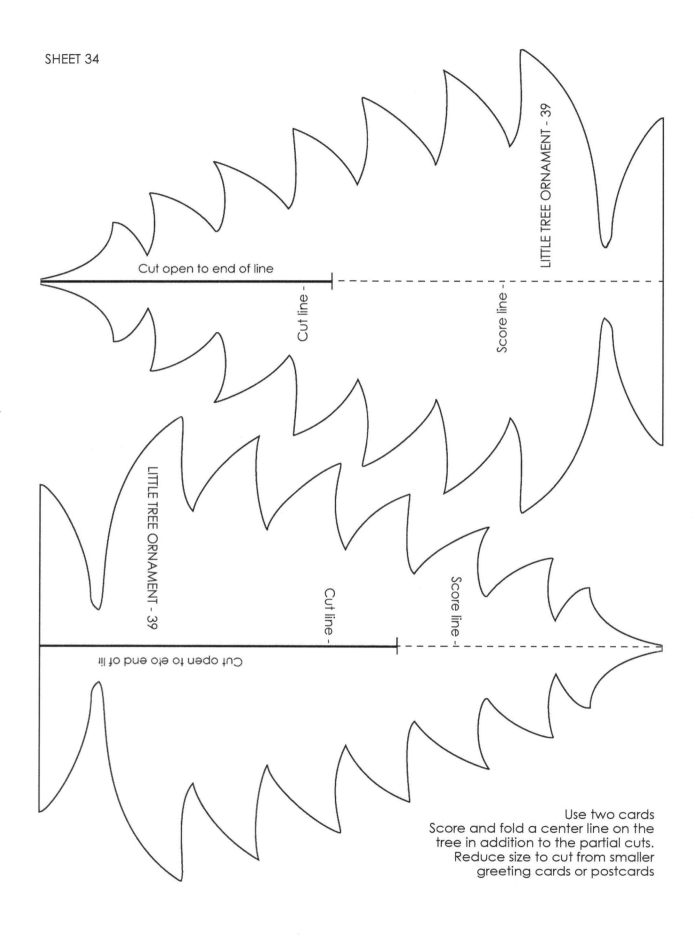

LITTLE TREE ORNAMENT - 39

Cut open to end of line

Cut line -

Score line -

LITTLE TREE ORNAMENT - 39

Cut line -

Score line -

Cut open to end of line

Use two cards
Score and fold a center line on the
tree in addition to the partial cuts.
Reduce size to cut from smaller
greeting cards or postcards

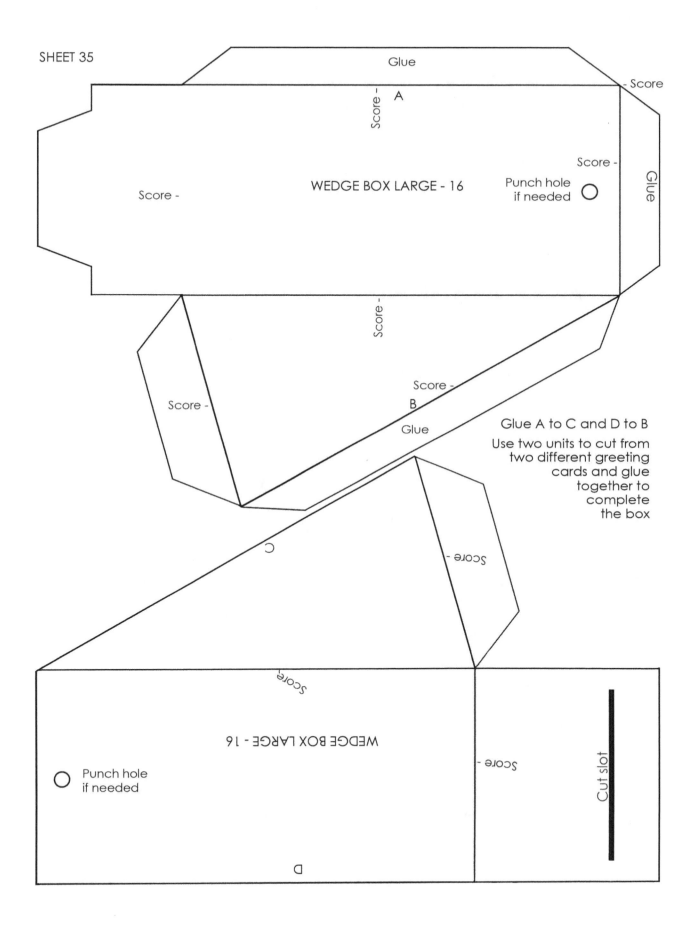

SHEET 35

Glue

- Score

Score -

A

Score -

WEDGE BOX LARGE - 16

Punch hole
if needed ○

Glue

Score -

Score -

Score -

Score -

B

Glue

Glue A to C and D to B

Use two units to cut from
two different greeting
cards and glue
together to
complete
the box

C

Score -

Score

WEDGE BOX LARGE - 16

○ Punch hole
if needed

Score -

Cut slot

D

SHEET 36

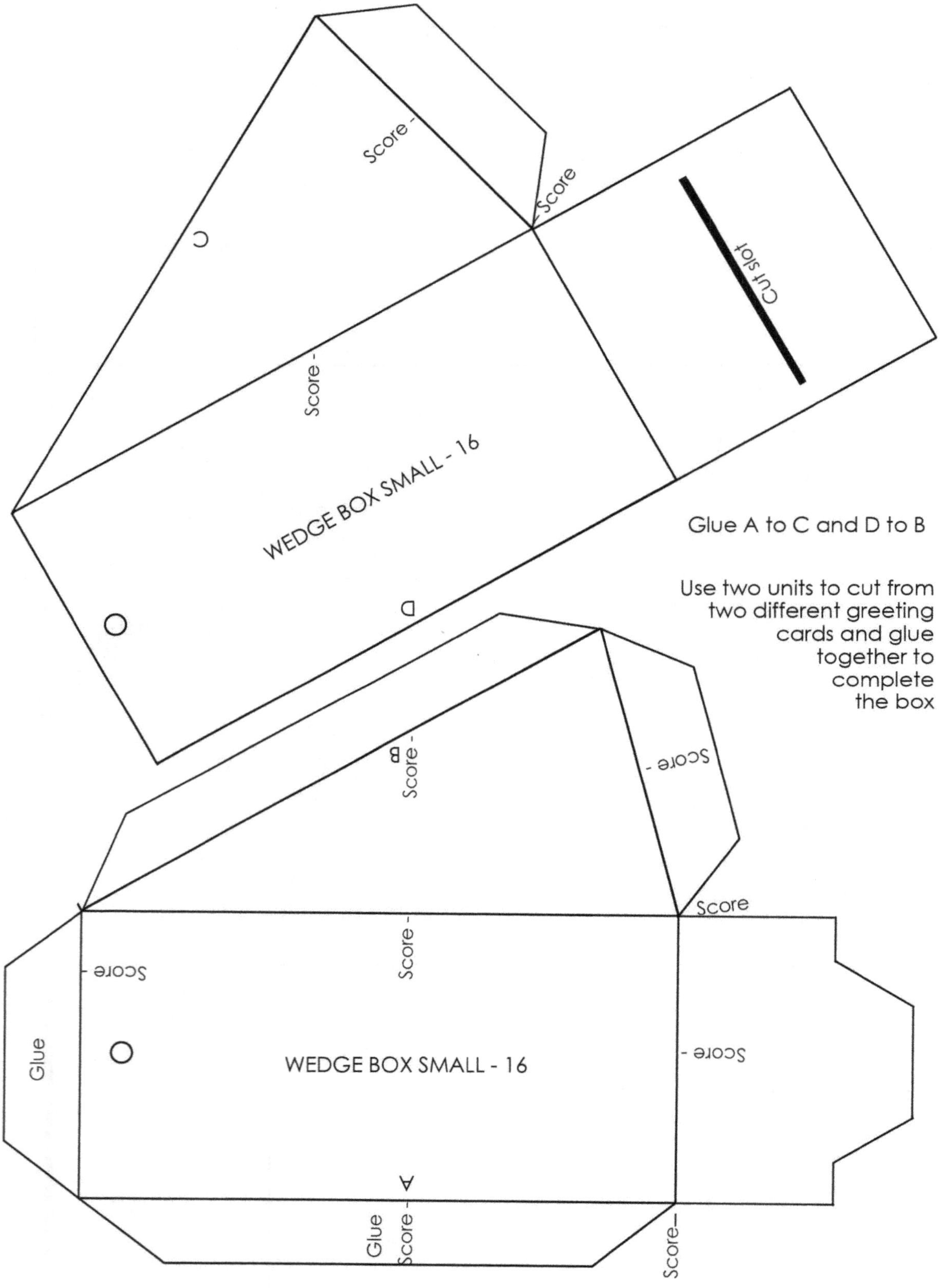
Score -
Score
C
Cut slot
Score -
WEDGE BOX SMALL - 16
D
B
Score -
Score -
Score
Score -
Score -
Glue
WEDGE BOX SMALL - 16
Score -
A
Score -
Glue
Score–

Glue A to C and D to B

Use two units to cut from two different greeting cards and glue together to complete the box

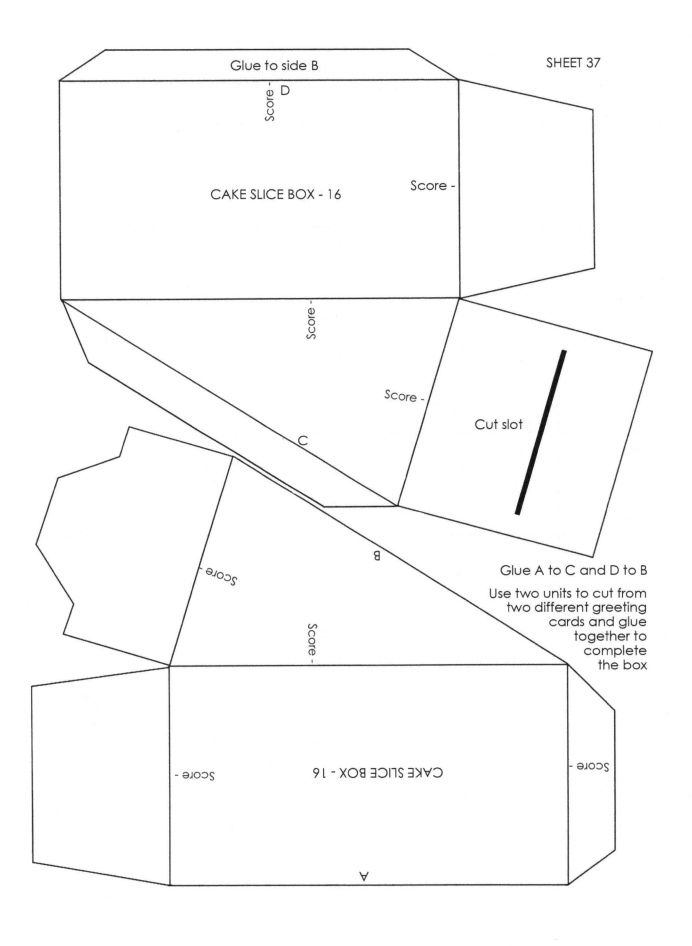

SHEET 37

Glue to side B

Score - D

CAKE SLICE BOX - 16

Score -

Score

Score -

Cut slot

C

Score

B

Glue A to C and D to B

Use two units to cut from
two different greeting
cards and glue
together to
complete
the box

Score -

CAKE SLICE BOX - 16

Score -

A

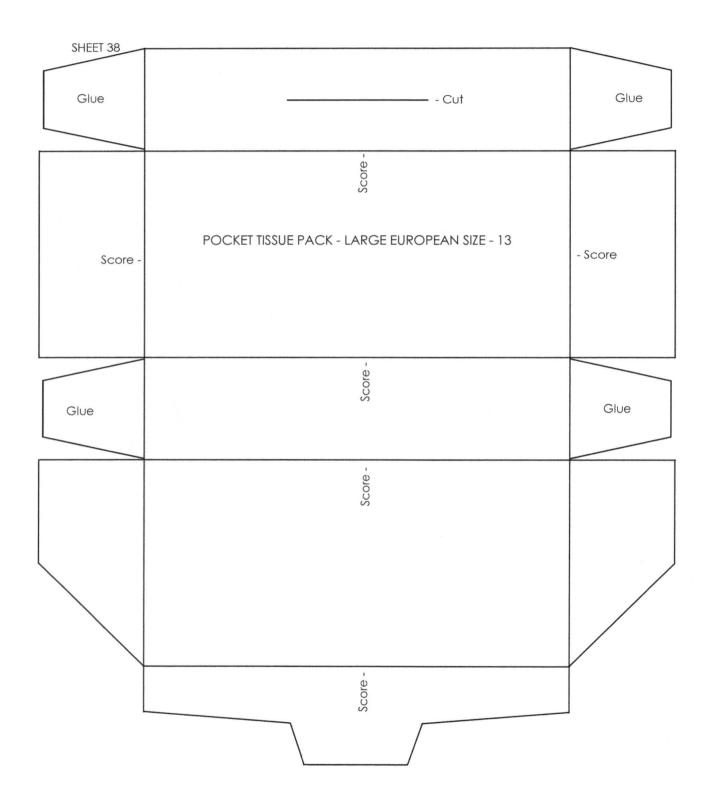

ADVENT NUMBERS FOR ADVENT POSTER - 46
Many other projects can be turned into Advent projects,
as well as countdown projects with seven days
Cut the numbers straight from this page or print from the printable template set

1	7	13	19
2	8	14	20
3	9	15	21
4	10	16	22
5	11	17	23
6	12	18	24